"Hammered Gold is an example of how tragedy can be turned into triumph for the glory of God. Rita captures the Biblical perspective on how to deal with heartache. This book stirred me emotionally and blessed me spiritually—a great read to comfort those who are hurting."

> Rev. Terry Herald
> Senior Associate Pastor , Whitesburg Baptist Church
> Huntsville, AL

"As I read Hammered Gold, I realized that I was seeing God at work in our world today. When I finished the last story, I wanted more. This is the encouragement we all need."

> Rev. Emerson Lyle
> Associate Pastor/Pastoral Care, Whitesburg Baptist Church
> Huntsville, AL

"Since I have been reading Hammered Gold, it has made me realize how easy it is to please God. I can devote myself to studying His Word and sharing my faith. God has used Hammered Gold to influence and change my life. "

> Amber Purser
> Huntsville, AL

Hammered

gold

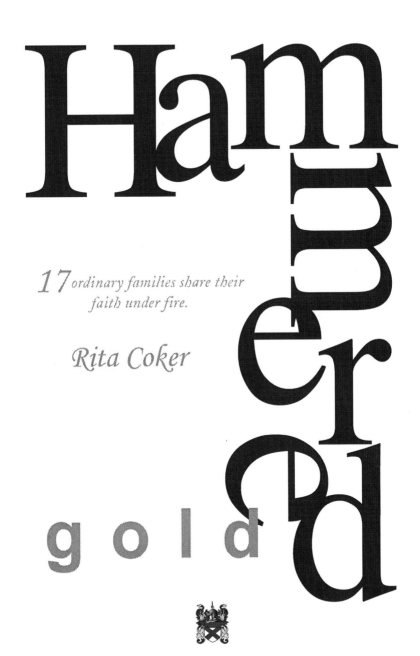

Hammered

17 ordinary families share their faith under fire.

Rita Coker

gold

TATE PUBLISHING & *Enterprises*

TATE PUBLISHING
& Enterprises

Tate Publishing is committed to excellence in the publishing industry. Our staff of highly trained professionals, including editors, graphic designers, and marketing personnel, work together to produce the very finest books available. The company reflects the philosophy established by the founders, based on Psalms 68:11,

"THE LORD GAVE THE WORD AND GREAT WAS THE COMPANY OF THOSE WHO PUBLISHED IT."

If you would like further information, please contact us:

1.888.361.9473 | www.tatepublishing.com

TATE PUBLISHING & *Enterprises*, LLC | 127 E. Trade Center Terrace

Mustang, Oklahoma 73064 USA

Hammered Gold

Book design copyright © 2007 by Tate Publishing, LLC. All rights reserved.

Cover design by Brandon Wood

Interior design by Jennifer Redden

Published in the United States of America

ISBN: 978-1-5988692-3-1

07.03.12

Seventeen testimonies
declare God's
faithfulness in the
midst of the fire.
Can your spirit sing when
your heart is broken?
Yes, if you understand that
God is too loving to be mean
And too wise to make a mistake.
From God's heart
To my heart
To your heart
With love.

Rita Coker
Matthew 11:28-30

This book is dedicated in memory of
Tiffany Leigh Stinson, our Granddaughter, a
precious gift from God for three joy-filled years.

Contents

A Personal Word from Rita

Never in our wildest dreams did we ever imagine what God had in mind for us in the writing of *From Silent Tears, the Hallelujah Song*. It took me three years to write, and then I thought it would maybe help our family members and friends who were hurting with us and rejoiced with us through the whole ordeal. The suddenness of the wreck and its devastating consequences was overwhelming to all of us. Young couples were terrified to put their children into their cars and go out into traffic for fear that this might happen to them. So I wrote what I thought would be a comfort to them in the days of adjusting ahead of them. But most of all, I wrote down as much as I could recall of all the events so that I could have a journal for Debbie to read when she was able to process the facts. It didn't seem fair that she was so physically impaired that she was not able to know from first hand experience what I felt she had a right to know. I elaborate on this in the book. But I also wrote down thoughts and emotions and fears that I experienced through it all. Since I could not get into someone's mind other than my own, it ends up being very first person.

The book was printed, and many people seemed so eager to

get their copy. It was not long before we realized that this was much bigger than we had anticipated. I would not attempt to try and tell you about all the responses we got from people even as far away as Alaska. One day I received a request from Auburn University's Library asking to obtain a copy. I'll just mention a few things that touched our hearts so deeply. One lady with very serious heart problems had just had her heart valves replaced. She was seriously depressed and didn't want to make an effort to get up and do anything. Her daughter bought her a copy of the book. She read it after her daughter went back to work. When the daughter got home, her mother was out of bed, dressed and saying she wanted to go shopping and out to eat. Can you imagine how God's Spirit must have worked in her spirit?

Then there was a handsome man in his forties going through a crisis in his marriage. He was so distraught, unable to eat or really function. He had lost over thirty pounds because of this depression. I had an opportunity to talk to him and gave him a copy of the book. The next evening I got a telephone call from him. His voice was so full of hope and joy. He said that when he reached the eighth chapter, he understood what he had to do. He chose to take the positive road and get up and move out focused on Jesus Christ, trusting Him to show him what to do from day to day.

There was another very special lady who had been diagnosed with cancer. They did not give her much hope for survival. She stopped me one day at church and thanked me for writing *From Silent Tears*. She expressed how she loved the way I had woven the church through the whole book. She also said out of all the books she had been given to read about illness and death, this was the one that helped her most to see victory in the midst of the crisis.

Now I haven't put names with these, but they will know who they are. There are literally hundreds more who expressed that they could see how we got through the wreck but they could not have done it. Tiffany's death, Debbie's and Garrett's injuries and long recuperation and rehabilitation seemed to be too much to bear. Our son-law Skip's accident in the middle of it when a big board hit him in the face, slicing his face open down the middle, added to the already heavy load. But we were constantly reminded that when the load got too weighty, all we had to do was reach around and there was a fresh new bundle of grace, just exactly what we needed right then. By faith we untied the bundle and praised God as the insurmountable grace poured out all over us. Now we could go on.

So when different ones would say, "You could do it, but I know we couldn't!" I knew I had to write another part to *From Silent Tears*. It's my way of answering by saying if you think you can't do what God says you can do with His help, then I'll show you a whole bunch of other testimonies of faithful Christians. You can see how they walked day by day with Jesus. Fiery trials came into their lives unexpectedly. Their faith walk was so consistent that they were able to see these circumstances as filtered through their heavenly Father's hands. Their spirit eyes had learned to delight in gazing on Him. Their spirit ears listened to His Word. Therein is the victory! Yes, and it is the victory in the midst of the fire! Oh, yes, and their spirits did sing even when their hearts were often broken!

After you read these testimonies, I pray that God will find hundreds more of his children who will always be found faithful, because God, our Father, is faithful! My prayer is that you will be one of them!

Now let me answer a few questions that some readers felt were left unanswered. About Debbie…."Did her face and body end up okay?" What a thrill it is for me to tell you that God did an awesome job of healing those horrible cuts on her face. Except for arthritic pain in cold or stormy weather, she has had no problem with her heel and ankle. She goes ninety miles an hour most of the time. She went back to college and got her Master's in Art Education and is now teaching in an elementary school.

We were told that she would not have full use of her left arm. It still has so much metal in it that she has to be careful about being out in a lightening storm. I'm kidding about that. I give so much credit to Laddie for being God's instrument in that particular rehabilitation. He was determined that she would use that arm. He knew that she would have to push past the place where she thought she could not handle anymore pain in order to get to the place where the arm would function. After three visits from the professional therapists in her home, they said that Laddie was doing the job as well or better than they could. Debbie trusted her father so completely to do only what would help her. That was a key. The end result is that she now has full use of the arm. It would be difficult for anyone to tell that her body had been so badly torn up if you looked at her today. There are still scars, but they don't capture your attention. It is her courage and strength and faith that mesmerize you.

Garrett has no obvious negative baggage as a result of his trauma at the tender age of five and a half. He is twenty-four now. You don't want this grandmother to start telling you about her grandson. It would take forever. Suffice it to say, he is the most handsome, intelligent, funny, talented, mischievous, wonderful little gift God ever gave to any family.

I had the privilege of sharing a short testimony in the Christmas Music Program at our church several years ago. Our music minister asked me to share something about the sustaining grace of God during the first Christmas after Tiffany's death. I shared the things that I included in *From Silent Tears* at the end of the letter I wrote to Tiffany. I told how we of course went on with Christmas because we still had Garrett, Debbie and Skip. Garrett came up to me at the end of the program and told me that his favorite part was when I said we still had Garrett. I said a hearty, "Yes, and that's my favorite part, too!" We really have been so blessed!

We have continued to buy a new ornament for the tree each year in memory of Tiffany. Some of my favorites are Precious Moments ornaments. One says, "May you have a heavenly Christmas." This encourages us to see Christmas with our spirit eyes from a heavenly perspective. Another one says, "I'll play my drum for you." This is a reminder for us to use every opportunity we have to give of ourselves to our Father in worship. Then there is one that says, "Tell me the story of Jesus." Tiffany is able to hear the Jesus story from Him personally. We must share His story in words and deeds until we join them in heaven. People need the Lord! The time must be near for His Coming again. May we all be found faithful!

Hammered Gold: God's Work

Realizing there would be a need for an explanation as to

why I chose *Hammered Gold* for the title of this book, I want to devote a chapter to unveiling the mystery.

There is a fascinating account in the Old Testament, I Kings 6:19ff, where King Solomon carries out God's instructions as to how He wants His Temple to be built.

> "And he, (Solomon), prepared the inner sanctuary inside the temple, to set the Ark of the Covenant of the Lord there. The inner sanctuary was twenty cubits long, twenty cubits wide, and twenty cubits high. He overlaid it with pure gold, and overlaid the altar of cedar with gold. So Solomon overlaid the inside of the temple with pure gold. He stretched gold chains across the front of the inner sanctuary, and overlaid it with gold. The whole temple he overlaid with gold, until he had finished all the temple; also he overlaid with gold the entire altar that was by the inner sanctuary."

The Macarthur Study Bible, page 482, offers John Macarthur's commentary: *"Gold was beaten into fine sheets, and then hammered to fit over the beautifully embellished wood (vv.18, 29), then attached to every surface in the temple proper, both in the Holy Place and in the Most Holy Place so that no wood or stone was visible (v. 22)."*

I inquired of a local jeweler about this process. He told me that when you subject gold to intense fire, you can then stretch it beyond what you can imagine. When the hammering is applied, the gold then becomes transparent, and at that point, its beauty shines forth as never before.

In I Corinthians 6:19, the Bible says:

> "Or do you not know that your body is the temple of the Holy Spirit who is in you, whom you have from God,

and you are not your own? For you were bought at a price, therefore, glorify God in your body, and in your spirit, which are God's."

This temple is so much more precious to God than a temple made with man made materials. The gold in Solomon's temple was incredibly beautiful and was admired by all who saw it. The gold that overlays the altar of God's child, his heart comes by way of trials and tribulations and testing. Through the most difficult circumstances, through the hottest fires, through the most turbulent waters, God is amazingly faithful to produce the transparent gold that allows Jesus Christ to shine through the testimonies of His faithful servants. And all who observe marvel at the work that only God Himself could accomplish.

Most people find themselves thinking, "Why, Lord?" when some painful trial appears at the door of their home. We need to understand that there is something positive about asking that question *if* it sends you to the Word of God to find answers. Let me share a few portions of scripture that might help you to know how to reason together with God through His Word.

> "My brethren, count it all joy when you fall into various trials, knowing that the testing of your faith produces patience. But let patience have its perfect work, that you may be perfect and complete, lacking nothing."
> James 1:2–4

First we need to understand the difference between joy and happiness. Happiness is dependent upon circumstances. Joy is dependent upon Jesus in you. When everything is going well, no major stress in your little world, you can be just as happy as a lark. When bad news comes, such as a serious illness or a death, or the teenager decides the time has come to drive their parents crazy with their rebellion, or your husband has his mid-life crisis, or your wife's hormones seem to turn her into someone you don't know, or the stock market crashes or whatever else you might think of, I guarantee you that you are not going to smile really big and say, "Wow, I have never been so happy!" But when God is ruling and reigning in your heart, He is ready in an instant to provide you with the peace and confidence you need to know that He is God, too wise to make a mistake and too loving to be mean. He is quite able to see you through this fire and take you to higher ground. Joy is contentment in the midst of circumstances because of Jesus. Through it all, He is working out His plan to conform you to the image of His Son, Jesus Christ, thereby perfecting or maturing you so that you find everything you need to keep you from stumbling is right there inside you—*Jesus in you in all his power and strength and glory!*

The apostle Peter says the same thing to us.

"In this you greatly rejoice, though now for a little while, if need be, you have been grieved by various trials, that the genuineness of your faith, being much more precious than gold that perishes, though it is tested by fire, may be found to praise, honor, and glory at the revelation of Jesus Christ." I Peter 1:6ff

The various manifold trials remind us that in each of our lives, trials are going to come. They will be different for each one of us. But the end result will be the same. If we receive the trial as from the Lord and embrace it, with the full knowledge that God has promised us that He will never leave us or forsake us, we will discover how carefully He keeps His word. He will surely walk through the fire with us. If it gets too much for us, He will carry us on His shoulder as a Good Shepherd carries a wounded sheep. Remember as our faith is tested, it is not so that God might know how deep our faith is, but rather that we ourselves will get a good look at just how real our faith is. This is crucial to our growth! God says in Isaiah 48:10b that He has tested us in the furnace of affliction.

Great comfort comes to us when the furnace of life's circumstances gets too hot, and we hear God speak to us again in Jeremiah 29:11–13:

> "For I know the thoughts that I think toward you, says the Lord, thoughts of peace and not of evil, to give you a future and a hope. Then you will call upon me and go and pray to me, and I will listen to you. And you will seek Me and find Me, when you search for me with all your heart."

When Satan whispers in your weary ears telling you that you can not survive your pain, please listen to God instead when He says in Isaiah 43:2–3:

> "When you pass through the waters, I will be with you; when you walk through the fire, you shall not be burned, nor shall the flame scorch you. For I am the Lord your God, The Holy One of Israel, your Savior."

Hallelujah! We don't have any confidence in our flesh, but we have all confidence in God who raises men from the dead! So as soon as the trial comes, we heed God's Word when He tells us in Hebrews 4:16:

> "Let us therefore come boldly to the throne of grace that

we may obtain mercy and find grace to help in the time of need."

There we find that God has indeed prepared for us the perfect Grace package to take care of every particular need that we might have. It is there for us in the time of need, not before the time of need. So don't spend energy trying to figure out how you would survive some other person's trial. You may never have to face that same circumstance. Just keep your eyes on Jesus day by day, and learn to trust Him in the little things, and then you will find it much easier to trust Him when the heavier trials come.

Having learned that trials are for the testing of our faith and are a tool to grow us, we must never forget that Satan would love nothing more than to use the same trial to pull us away from God. If he can convince us that God is being mean to us or that we have a right to be so angry with God so that we want nothing more to do with Him, he has won that battle for your mind. One thing we know is that when you listen to Satan's lies, you will always be one defeated, depressed and ultimately destroyed mess. Satan's objective where we are concerned is to ruin our lives. God, on the other hand, in His amazing love for us, desires to use every event in our lives to draw us to Himself where He can show us that He has already provided for us all that we have need of pertaining to life and godliness. He wants to gather us under His wings and shelter us in the midst of the fire and storm. He wants to raise us up to a higher place than we have ever been. He wants to reveal to us His plan for a special ministry that He will perform through us that will glorify His name as we reach out and touch others with godly comfort and wisdom.

Therefore, these various trials are permitted in our lives for the testing of our faith and as a tool to grow us in the grace and knowledge of our Lord Jesus Christ. We learn the necessity of looking at our circumstances with spirit eyes, and there we see that we are never alone. He is always there, and where He is, there is joy and peace. We find that as we open His word, we are able to listen to Him with our spirit ears, and we are amazed at how clearly He speaks to our hearts with words of comfort and how step by step guidance is given to us. Worship and praise seem to flow as our hearts rejoice in His presence. Now we know that we can receive the trial and embrace it because it is an opportunity, and yes, a privilege, to be trusted with a testing that will bring forth pure gold that will reflect and glorify our Father.

That brings us to a second thing we learn about a trial. Once we have gone through the fire, the gold has been hammered and it covers the altar of our hearts, the reflection of Jesus shines through the countenance of His child; He tells us that He has a special ministry for us. In II Corinthians1: 3–4, the Holy Spirit inspired Paul to write this to us out of his own experience.

> "Blessed be the God and Father of our Lord Jesus Christ, the Father of mercies and God of all comfort, who comforts us in all our tribulation, that we may be able to comfort those who are in any trouble, with the comfort with which we ourselves are comforted by God."

As we go through the difficult circumstances in our lives, the Comforter, who is the Holy Spirit, is in us recalling to our memory precious promises in God' word. He is praying for us when we can't seem to find the words to express our own prayers. His strength is perfect when we feel that we have no strength at all. He surrounds us with godly people to minister to us using their various spiritual gifts. Prayers of others, some we do not even know, lift us up to the throne of God. I could go on and on, but suffice it to say that all of this comfort God leaves with us, so that on down the road somewhere, we will find someone else with a broken heart, and we can reach out to them and share this blessed comfort with them.

In Psalm 84:5–7, we are given the same insight into this ministry aspect of testing.

> "Blessed is the man whose strength is in You (God), whose heart is set on pilgrimage. As they pass through the Valley of Baca, they make it a spring. The rain also covers it with pools. They go from strength to strength; each one appears before God in Zion."

"Baca" means weeping or sorrow. As they passed through this dry and thirsty place on their way to Zion, they chose to dig a well. Out of that well came fresh water that would not only meet their need, but would also be there for others passing through their Valley of Sorrow. They made an arid valley into a place of joy. The strength they derive from this ministry of sharing causes them to overcome the weariness and depression that would otherwise paralyze them. They are set free to rejoice in the Lord in all things!

Can you see, then, how trials produce powerful testimonies? Don't you long to have a testimony that lifts up Jesus and glorifies our Father's name? Listen to what Job said after he had been tested to the max. Satan thought Job was a faithful servant of God's because God had blessed him so abundantly. But you see, Satan doesn't know nearly as much as he thinks he does. God is all-knowing and knew He could trust Job in all kinds of circumstances. God agreed to let Satan attack Job and take everything from him except his life. Through the loss of his children, his wealth, and his health, Job just kept on loving and trusting God. Read the book of Job for yourself, but let me just whisk you on over to the end of the book and the most important thing that Job said. His testimony was as follows:

> "I know that You can do everything, and that no purpose of Yours can be withheld from You. You asked, "Who is this who hides counsel with knowledge?" Therefore I have uttered what I did not understand, things too wonderful for me, which I did not know. Listen, please, and let me speak; You said, "I will question you, and you shall answer Me." I have heard of You by the hearing of the ear, but now my eye sees You. Therefore, I abhor myself and repent in dust and ashes." Job 42:1–6

Listen now to Paul express his heart as to what is really important in a testimony.

> "But what things were gain to me, these I have counted loss for Christ. Yet indeed I also count all things loss for the excellence of the knowledge of Christ Jesus my Lord, for whom I have suffered the loss of all things, and count them as rubbish, that I may gain Christ and be found in Him, not having my own righteousness, which is from the law, but that which is through faith in Christ, the righteousness which is from God by faith; that I may know Him and the power of His resurrection and the fellowship of His sufferings, being conformed to His death, if, by any means, I may attain to the resurrection from the dead." Philippians 3:7–10

Centuries separated the lives of these two men. Paul had so

much more insight into God's Son's finished work on Calvary's cross than did Job. But God was able to speak as clearly to Job's spirit as He did to Paul's. No wealth, health, title or reputation could ever compare to the experience they had when they *saw God* through their trials.

Peter summed it up so beautifully when he said:

"In this, you greatly rejoice, though now for a little while, if need be, you have been grieved by various trials, that the genuineness of your faith, being much more precious than gold, that perishes, though it is tested by fire, may be found to praise, honor and glory at the revelation of Jesus Christ, whom having not seen you love. Though now you do not see Him, yet believing, you rejoice with joy inexpressible and full of glory, receiving the end of your faith - the salvation of your souls." I Peter 1:6-9

What we all rejoice in is that we have been born again to a living hope through the resurrection of Jesus Christ from the dead. Now we have an inheritance incorruptible and undefiled and that does not fade away. It is reserved in heaven for us who are kept by the power of God through faith for salvation ready to be revealed in the last time. *What a testimony!*

Personal testimonies spoken from the hearts of individuals who have gone through their trials in victory are more powerful than sermons preached from a pulpit. Paul is an example for us to follow. II Corinthians is the letter he writes where he pours out his heart about what God has taught him through experience. In the eleventh chapter, verses 7-10, he shares the most amazing insight into why God does not always deliver us from suffering.

"And lest I should be exalted above measure by the abundance of the revelations, a thorn in the flesh was given to me, a messenger of Satan to buffet me, lest I be exalted above measure. Concerning this thing I pleaded with the Lord three times that it might depart from me. And He said to me, "My grace is sufficient for you, for My strength is made perfect in weakness." Therefore most gladly, I will rather boast in my infirmities, that the power of Christ may rest upon me. Therefore I take pleasure in infirmities, in reproaches, in needs, in persecutions, in distresses, for Christ's sake. For when I am weak, then I am strong."

We are never more aware of the inadequacy of our flesh than we are in the midst of a fiery trial. It is humbling to have to admit that so many things that happen to us are beyond our control. So we know we have to cease to have confidence in our flesh and remember that we can have all confidence in God who raises men from the dead. We turn to Him, yielding our wills to His will and eager to accept whatever He knows will be for our good and His glory. He does not always remove the trial, but His promise is that He will be right there with us supplying the continuing grace needed to meet our every need. The weaker we are the more clearly God's grace shows through us. That's the process of hammering the gold. God stretches the gold, hammers the gold and overlays the altar of our hearts. In its transparency, Jesus Christ shines through our eyes, and our countenance is illuminated so that all who observe God's child are drawn to God's Son, Jesus Christ.

I'd like to share one more testimony from the Old Testament. Joseph, the pampered and beloved son of Jacob, lived what we call the "good life." His circumstances changed drastically when the hate and jealousy of his brothers manifested itself in the most cruel way one day when Joseph was least expecting it. The desire of the hearts of these dysfunctional siblings was to see Joseph dead. God did not permit them to kill Joseph. But they did sell him to strangers who took him to Egypt. Please take the time to read the entire story of how God's blessing was on Joseph all through his captivity. Because Joseph stayed faithful to God, God saw that he was continually finding favor with these strangers. The day came when, as a result of a famine throughout the land, the brothers were forced to come to Egypt to see if they could buy grain so that their families might survive. Never in their wildest dreams did they imagine that their brother could have possibly been exalted to the position of the second most powerful man in Egypt. Ultimately Joseph unveiled his identity. Fear filled the hearts of the brothers as they remembered what they had done to Joseph. Genesis 50:18–21 sums up the victorious testimony of Joseph.

> "Then his brothers also went and fell down before his face, and they said, "Behold, we are your servants." Joseph said to them, "Do not be afraid, for am I in the place of God? But as for you, you meant evil against me, but God meant it for good, in order to bring it about as it is this day, to save many people alive. Now therefore, do not be afraid. I will provide for you and your little ones." And he comforted them and spoke kindly to them.

Do you see the hammered gold? Only God can produce such loving kindness and forgiveness and generosity in Joseph's life and in ours. This kind of testimony will be used by God to save many lost and hurting souls. That is the reason I wrote this book.

As you read each of the testimonies included here, my prayer is that your life will be forever changed as you see time and again the faithfulness of God in ordinary people's lives. Their trials are uniquely different. The common threads that run through each ones experiences are that they all know and love Jesus Christ personally, they all believe the Bible is the inspired Word of God, and they all find their source of strength in the intimate time they spend with God through prayer daily.

May we all go and do likewise!

Book I

From Silent Tears the Hallelujah Song

Introduction

"Now the Word of the Lord came to me saying, before I formed you in the womb I knew you, and before you were born I consecrated you; I have appointed you a prophet to the nations." Jeremiah 1:4–5

Imagine that! God, who spoke the universe into existence, knows each individual before we are conceived. Not only does He know us, but He has a plan for each of our lives. It is a good thing for us that He does not lay the whole life span out on a chart for us to read. We would not be able to mentally and emotionally handle seeing all the mountains and the valleys in our future.

God reveals His will for us one day, even one step, at a time. Obedience takes us to the next step. Disobedience and rebellion stops us from progressing forward. Sometimes gently and lovingly God shows us the wisdom of denying self and following after Him. Many times, the chastening hand of God comes to bear upon our stiff-necked attitudes. Still with love, He convinces us to turn from our wicked ways, confess our sins, and walk with Him on down that blessed Calvary Road. There is where we find grace we need in that time of crisis.

Early on, we, like Jeremiah, realize that even those who commit their lives to God do not find that life is a continual bed of roses. We discover soon that the rain falls on the just and the unjust, and the sun shines on the just and the unjust. Some of God's children, when subjected to the sudden trials that interrupt their otherwise orderly lives, can identify with Jeremiah's pity parties. In the twentieth chapter of Jeremiah, verses fourteen through eighteen, listen to his doubting heart.

> "Cursed be the day when I was born;
> Let the day not be blessed when my mother bore me!
> Cursed be the man who brought the news
> To my father, saying
> "A baby boy has been born to you!"
> And made him very happy.
> But let the man be like the cities
> Which the Lord overthrew
> without relenting.
> And let him hear an outcry in the morning.
> And a shout of alarm at noon;
> Because he did not kill me before birth,
> So that my mother would have been my grave,
> And her womb ever pregnant.
> Why did I ever come forth from the womb
> To look on trouble and sorrow,
> So that my days have been spent in shame?

Have you ever felt like things had pressed in on you from every side? Does it seem that as you cry out for deliverance, all of creation, including God, has temporarily lost their ability to hear? As you attempt to take matters into your own hands and find your own way of escape, do you rather discover that the best of your own wise devices seem to cause you to sink deeper into despair and desperation? Hopefully, you did not spend a lot of energy cursing your birthday and wishing that your mother would be forever with a pregnant stomach!

How much healthier it is to go on over to Jeremiah 29:11–13.

"For I know the plans that I have for you," declares the Lord, "plans for welfare and not for calamity to give you a future and a hope. Then you will call upon Me and come and pray to Me and find Me, and I will listen to you. And you will seek Me and find Me, when you search for Me with all your heart."

God told Jeremiah from the start that He had a plan for him. Circumstances, people and things stole from him his concentration. In his distraction, he got his eyes off God and onto his problems. Soon his attitude revealed his root of bitterness. From his pool of self-pity, he blamed everybody for his misery.

Are we not guilty of doing the very same thing? Point the finger at your parents if you are lacking discipline in your own life. A spouse is a convenient excuse for our giving in to our own desire to satisfy our own flesh. If they had met our every need, we would have been perfectly content. Blame the church, the pastor, the staff, the teachers, or the church mice if you can't find anyone else for your laziness when it comes to serving the Lord and worshipping the Lord together with believers.

Charles Spurgeon said, "The Lord gets his best soldiers out of the highlands of affliction." God has always permitted His children to go through experiences of suffering. As gold is strengthened as it is put through the fire, so we are made stronger as we endure the hammering trials that come our way. God chooses what we go through. We choose how we go through it. Without God's enabling power, we will fail each and every time. With God's presence and power and grace, we will rejoice in the knowledge that man's extremity is God's opportunity to show His ability to do above and beyond anything we ever hoped or dreamed. As He protected Daniel from the hungry lions; as he prevented the fire in the super heated furnace from singeing one hair on Shadrach, Meschack and Abednego's bodies; so He is able to provide a way of escape for us and meet every need that we have according to His riches in glory by Christ Jesus.

I pray that this humble effort at putting thoughts and truths on paper will lift up Jesus, edify his children and bring glory to our Father's Name. Without Him, I would not have survived the heartbreaking trials that have come my way. With Him, I have learned that He is able to keep me from falling. His strength is more than sufficient for all my needs.

I am resting in the person and the promises and the provisions and protection of the One who raises men from the dead. How could I fail to overcome? And overcoming, how can I keep my heart from singing and my lips from praising His holy name?

I. *The Unexpected Call*

Almost one year had passed since my husband Laddie opted for an early retirement from the Missile Command at Redstone Arsenal in Huntsville, Alabama. On May 1, 1987, he was like a bird released from a cage.

We had longed for the day when we could put our feet up, sip lemonade, and throw stress to the wind.

Just prior to retirement, he started the biggest project of his life. He put in an in-ground 18' X 36' swimming pool. Except for digging the hole and dynamiting the rock (we live at the foot of a mountain), he tackled and completed the project in nine months. He even bought an electric concrete mixer and made the concrete that covered the entire area around the pool inside the fence. Skip Stinson, our son-in-law, contributed his "brawn" when they came for weekend visits from Birmingham, Alabama.

When the pool was ready to be filled with water, my two grandchildren, Garrett, five, and Tiffany, two, joined me as we took our places on the steps. We waited patiently as the water started to rise up on us. Of course, at this point, there was still dirt around the edge of the pool. So, it was a bit muddy getting out, and a whole lot of cold sitting in the water, but what did we care? We had a big swimming pool. And we were as happy as little kids in a candy store.

Now we had one other big project that had to be done. The fence around the pool had to be painted. One thing calls for another. The painted fence showed up the need for the house to get a fresh coat of paint.

Okay, so we would rest and enjoy our retirement *after* the painting jobs were completed.

It was Monday, May 23, 1988. Laddie worked very hard helping to construct a Brush Arbor for a two-night revival. In case you have never heard of a Brush Arbor, let me see if I can explain its origin.

As the settlers went west looking for places to settle down, build houses, plant gardens, and build a future for their families, they would stop at intervals and regroup. They would often take wood and erect a simple frame and fill in the top with brush.

The preaching took place under the arbor while the families sat around on the ground. They never wanted to forget to worship and praise God for His watch-care over them.

Now that's what we did once a year at Whitesburg Baptist Church. In the simplest surroundings, we remembered the faith of our fathers. And we acknowledge that in spite of the fact that we live in the Space Capital of the United States, and our church is "chock full" of engineers and scientists and so on, we are still just as desperately in need of God's touch and His grace and His mercy as those pioneers were. And so we pray and praise and preach the "old time" religion. All men have heartache caused by sin. All men need help. All men find help and salvation in Jesus Christ.

Sunday night, May 22, the rain began to fall. Now that can

put a damper on a Brush Arbor. No one complained about rain because Alabama had suffered from a very long drought.

So we just changed our plans and had the first *indoor* Brush Arbor. God blessed! Souls were saved! God's people rejoiced and looked forward to Monday night.

Monday was a day filled with excitement. Laddie was asked to give a little testimony at the meeting. He spent a lot of time getting what he wanted to share condensed into two minutes worth.

I studied for my last Bible study of the year. Our Tuesday Ladies' Bible Study at Whitesburg Baptist Church had been studying Jeremiah for two years. By the time we concluded the study, we all understood better why he was called the Weeping Prophet.

Our anniversary brunch was planned for the next morning. We all looked forward to this time once a year. You knew there would be good food (spiritual and physical), and good fellowship and fun.

My friend, Brenda McDaniel is always reaching out to people in need. John Strickland worked for the city of Huntsville for many years, as did Brenda. She began to minister to the Strickland's when Mrs. Strickland was terminally ill.

After Mrs. Strickland died, Brenda continued to help Strick with business details, trips to doctors and hospitals, grocery shopping and other things.

One day Brenda asked me to go with her and talk to Strick and see if I could get a sense of whether or not he was born again.

I went to visit him two or three times. His sister, Olivia, came to live with him. Both of them were unable to take care of themselves.

Strick had died on Saturday, and the funeral was at eleven

o' clock on Monday morning. So much was going on, I almost forgot about the funeral service.

I felt that since he was not a member of a church, there would be a small gathering of friends at the funeral home. He and Olivia had but a handful of family members. There were not any brothers and sisters.

Feeling impressed to be a physical presence there; I got dressed and went, even though I knew I had a million things to do.

As I had expected, the crowd was small. I sat alone for awhile. In the stillness, I began to reflect upon how sad it was not to be surrounded by a church family and your own pastor. One of our staff members was asked to share the message. It was very evangelistic. There was not too much he could say about the man as he hardly knew him.

I began to feel so thankful for my salvation and my church family and for our staff members. I was filled with gratitude for my family. I remember thanking the Lord that if one of my family members died that day, I would not have to wonder where they would go. How peaceful it was to know we all had been born again. As for our grandchildren, there was that blessed assurance that they were safely cradled in God's amazing grace until they came to the age of accountability recognizing that they were sinners in need of God's salvation.

I left after the service and went on about the day's business, not knowing how this particular experience would be brought to my mind before the day ended.

Laddie had painted until about four in the afternoon. I reminded him of the meeting and that we needed to be there before six o'clock. He cleaned his brush, put away paint and ladder, and began to get himself cleaned up.

The telephone rang. I answered and was surprised to hear our son-in-law's voice. "Rita," he said, in a very serious tone, "Deb's been in a terrible car wreck, and she's hurt real bad." Debbie is our only child.

My heart sank. "What about the children? Are they going to be okay?"

"Debbie's broken up and cut up real bad, but they think she's going to be alright. They took her by helicopter to the Trauma Center at Caraway Methodist Hospital. They took the children to Children's Hospital."

"We'll be there as soon as we can!" I hung up the receiver and felt as though I would be sick. My legs were weak, and my head was spinning. Birmingham is at least an hour and a half south of Huntsville, and we needed to be with them *now*.

"Debbie and the kids have been in a bad car accident!" I blurted out to Laddie. "We've got to get to Caraway in a hurry!"

What do I do first? *Think!* Stop and think! Call the church! The line was busy! Call Brenda and Ray! They could call others for us and could get prayer warriors praying.

Their daughter, Sonja, answered the phone. She was so sweet, as usual. How I hated to give such bad news to her. Brenda and Ray were not at home.

"Sonja, please call the church for us!" and I told her what we knew.

We had no idea where the hospital was. Remembering that Doni Harrison had spent months there with her mother, I called her. I worried about her because she and Debbie were so close. Also, Doni, Bo and their children had been in a very serious car accident only a year and a half before. I knew she would be devastated. I called and she had Bo call back with directions.

In the meantime, Ray called back to offer to drive us down or to help with anything we might need.

Marilyn Calvert called to offer to drive us down. Laddie knew that we would have to have our car, since we had no idea how long we would be staying.

I ran next door to tell the Clarks so that someone in the neighborhood would know where we were. It was drizzling rain. No one was at home.

I ran back to our house, up the stairs, and began to throw things into a suitcase. I knew we could need any number of different things, but I couldn't think rationally. So I just randomly threw things in. Somehow, it didn't seem to matter.

Everything took so long. Laddie seemed to be moving in slow motion. We got into the car finally, and it was almost out of gas. We were out of money so we had to go by the Anytime Teller at the bank. Every light turned red as soon as we approached it.

I prayed so hard. "Dear Father, how we need your peace to saturate our minds and emotions. Please comfort our children! Wrap them in your warm blanket of love!"

As I prayed, I felt His love as He gently began to calm my spirit.

After a long period of silence, Laddie and I agreed that from the way Skip had worded the brief conversation, Debbie was in the most critical condition. Broken bones would mend, and plastic surgery would take care of the cuts. Garrett and Tiffany would recover. Children are strong and bounce back so quickly. Somehow we managed to convince ourselves that we had let our imaginations run wild.

Laddie got behind an eighteen-wheeler, and we sped down

I-65 at ninety miles an hour. Bo had given good directions, and we got to Caraway in record time.

Rushing into a strange hospital was very intimidating. We had no idea where we should go to find Skip. As we rushed through unfamiliar halls, we inquired of uniformed strangers for directions to the Emergency Room.

Finally, we saw a nurses' station and a short man with his back to us. He turned, and much to our surprise, we recognized a dear friend who had grown up in our church with Debbie. Jeff Flinn was the Chaplain on duty that evening. He hugged us so tightly and led us into an empty waiting room.

"Let me fill you in on what is going on now," he said. "Debbie is in surgery. She will be there for several more hours. She was badly broken up… an elbow, a knee, and a heel was crushed, and they were all open traumas. They'll have to tediously get all the debris out of these wounds to try and prevent infection. A wrist and an ankle were broken. There are many cuts and abrasions on her legs. Her face is cut up really bad. As far as they can tell, there are no internal injuries. That's the best news we have for you. Dr. Bromberg is the orthopedic surgeon. He's the best in this field. He says she's going to make it, barring infections."

It was like a heavy load had been lifted off us. She was going to live. We were sure that everything else would work out.

Jeff continued. "Skip is at Children's Hospital with Garrett and Tiffany. Garrett has a pretty big cut down the side of his face and some cuts in the top of his head. He also has a small fracture in one hip that they believe will heal itself quickly. His prognosis is very good."

Once again, we felt such enormous relief.

Then Jeff's face became so somber, and he said, "Tiffany is

hurt the worst! She's on a life support machine. The impact of the crash snapped two vertebrae in her neck. One cut off her breathing, and the other stopped her heart. The paramedics worked with her and got the heart started back beating and put her on a respirator. But she is brain dead."

No! No! Not Tiffany. She's only three. She's just started her life. She's so energetic and bouncy. She can't die! Laddie and I both sobbed.

"Since Debbie will be in surgery for many hours, I would suggest you go to Children's Hospital to be with Skip. He needs you now."

He told us about being with Skip when he got to Caraway after being called at work and told about the accident. In ministering to a man in shock, he asked Skip to tell him about his family. Skip took a picture from his wallet that Laddie had made about six months earlier. Jeff asked, "Is this Debbie Coker?"

What a special touch of loving kindness, surely from God himself. He had placed this sensitive, godly friend in that spot twice, once for Skip and a second time for Laddie and me. We were reminded early that God was in charge of our circumstances. He would indeed take care of each one of us.

We then rushed to Children's Hospital. We made our way up to the third floor. Many friends and co-workers filled the hall. Skip was inside a waiting room with his father, Bob, and Augusta, his wife. Their pastor and some other relatives were there.

That two hundred fifty-pound massive man wrapped his arms around me and wept openly. "I'm losing my little girl!" he sobbed. My heart broke. Nothing had prepared me for the pain I felt in my soul. "I'm so sorry! I'm so sorry! I'm so sorry!" I heard myself repeating this same thing over and over. I looked across the room and saw Laddie crying. There had been very few times I'd seen him cry. We all loved this little girl so very much. Everything in us felt that it should have been one of us. We had already lived such full lives. She was only beginning. "Please, God, let her live!" was our supplication. It seemed that there were moments of peace followed by moments of panic for the rest of the evening. The uncertainty about what the outcome would be was awesome.

As we waited, God brought many friends to comfort us. At one point, we looked up and saw the Karrs and the Calverts, close friends from Huntsville, who stayed most of the night with us.

A lady came into the room who we didn't recognize. She introduced herself as Jo Taylor. She said she told her husband she could not go to bed until she came to the hospital to tell us she was driving the car behind Debbie. She wanted us to know that Debbie was in no way at fault. She was driving under the speed limit, straight down the middle of her lane. She did not even have a chance to put on her brakes as the pickup truck came into her lane. The truck had been driven by a young sixteen-year-old high school student who had had his driver's license for only two weeks and did not have the experience to drive in this sudden rainstorm with hazardous oil on the long dried pavement.

Jo wanted us to know that everything that possibly could have been done for our children was done, at the risk of many people's safety. The car was smoking. They feared it would explode.

She shared with us how she had stayed close to Debbie, who was fully conscious, and talked to her to keep her calm. Jo went though Debbie's purse and couldn't find Skip's business number. The checkbook was used by Jo to call the bank and get his number.

I knew God had placed Jo there that day. She was so calm and so gentle. I thanked God for her. She told me how she had prayed and wept for Debbie, Tiffany and Garrett.

After some time had passed, knowing Skip was in good hands, Laddie and I went back to Caraway to wait for Debbie to come out of surgery.

The word finally came in the early hours of the morning that we could see her as they rolled her to the Intensive Care Unit. Her eyes were covered with wide bandages, her mouth so swollen, casts on arms and legs. I was devastated, but so thankful she was alive.

"Hi, Honey!" I choked back the tears.

"Hi, Mom, is Tiffany okay?" Then she asked if Tiffany was dead.

"Tiffany and Garrett are at Children's Hospital. The best doctors are taking care of them. Skip is with them. Try not to worry. We'll be here for you. We won't leave. We love you, Honey!"

Laddie and I did our best to comfort each other. Our emotions were out of control. We never knew anything could hurt like this. Our only child, our only two grandchildren—how close we had come to losing all three of them.

Each time we visited Debbie in ICU, she asked about Garrett, but specifically about Tiffany. She would ask if Tiff were still alive, as though she knew in her heart that she was not. We kept saying she was on a life support system, and it didn't look good.

Dr. Bromberg, the orthopedic surgeon, met with us to tell us about the extent of Debbie's injuries. There was a shattered left elbow that had two pieces of bone missing. With screws and bolts and wire, he had put it back together but wasn't sure as to how much use she would have of it. The right wrist was broken. The right leg was messed up badly—a shattered kneecap, broken ankle (the foot was turned around), and a crushed heel. He said it looked like crushed corn flakes, and he wasn't really pleased with the outcome or the prognosis.

He told us that her young age was in her favor. Had she been older, this kind of trauma would have killed her.

He finished with this uncertain picture, not at all what we had hoped to hear.

I found myself answering him. "You don't know our daughter! She's strong mentally, emotionally, physically and spiritually. She heals well. Broken bones mend, and cuts heal. She has a deep faith in God and many people are praying for her. She'll come through this better than you think!"

He retorted, "Well, I guess it's good to believe in a higher being." His shallow response convinced me that he had missed my point.

I said, "It's more personal than that. Our daughter knows his name. His name is Jesus Christ."

He came back with, "Well, Job asked why."

"We don't have to ask why. God is too loving to be mean and too wise to make a mistake. We trust Him to work this out for good as He said He would."

He obviously did not understand our simple faith and confidence in God.

2. *Tiffany is not Here*

Tuesday we got a call to join Skip right away. Nothing could be done for Tiffany. They had to disconnect her from the life support machine lines. A decision had to be made about donating Tiffany's organs.

We made our way again to Children's Hospital. Laddie let me out before he parked so that I could go on to Skip.

A security guard noticed me as I was trying to figure out what would be the fastest route.

He noticed that I was crying. He left his station and came to me. "Stop that crying," he said rather sharply.

"I can't help it," I sobbed. "My little three-year-old granddaughter is going to be taken off the life support system in a little while. I need to get to my son-in-law."

"You should have stayed in the car with your husband. Then you could have gone to the right floor from the upper parking tier," his voice was scolding.

"I just thought maybe I could get there sooner from here," I sobbed.

"Come on, I'll take you to him." He talked non-stop, telling me how God was sparing our baby from having to live her life in this messed-up world. He told me how much hate he had experienced serving in three wars, and the cultural oppression, and on and on he went.

When he got me to the right floor, he said, "Now, I don't want you to think I'm not sensitive to your pain. I'm going to pray for you and your family. God's gonna take care of you."

With eyes full of tears, and a much calmer spirit, I thanked this dear man for being one of the people God had placed at just the right time when I needed His special touch. Surely, he was an angel unaware.

Skip had made his decision, after great agonizing, and signed the papers for the representative of the Transplant Foundation. We became very aware of how important it is for families to discuss this matter and come to their decision before the crisis comes.

They let him go into the room with Tiffany and hold her and rock her still cold body until he felt free to release her. No one but God could know how broken and empty he must have felt at that moment.

Of course, she had been brain dead from the time of the accident. But it must have been so hard for him to give up that beautiful little body.

So much had to be done. Skip's father had a crypt next to where his mother was buried. He wanted Tiffany to be buried there. Skip was so thankful. Not just for the provision, but that her body would be so close to where they had placed his mother's body.

I offered to go to Huntsville and make all the arrangements, as Skip needed to stay with Garrett day and night.

Jane and Barbara, my two sisters, had gotten to Birmingham Tuesday. They went with me to Huntsville Wednesday night.

Before I left, I went in to see Debbie. "Mama, has Tiffany died?" she asked one last time.

"Yes, Honey, she has." "I need to talk to you about some things I have in mind for her service. I need your thoughts and approval." She was so very calm. I don't know if we could have handled it had she completely fallen apart. God had her so wrapped in His loving grace; it was truly amazing grace. Her eyes had been filled with glass. I knew God had held many salty tears back to protect her eyes.

I told her about having the service at our church. Brother Jimmy Jackson, our pastor, would have the message, and Brother Herman, Skip and Debbie's pastor, would share some thoughts about Tiffany. Debbie liked that.

"I've chosen that pretty little white organdy dress with the pink satin ribbon," I said.

"Don't forget her slip and panty hose and white Sunday school shoes! And put one of her dressy ribbons in her hair, Mama."

Laddie had to leave the room. His heart was so broken. Tiffany's death had devastated him. Then to see his own child, in such a fragile physical state, having to face the emotional trauma of losing her own baby, and unable even to be a part of the plans for her service—it seemed too much to bear.

I assured Debbie that I would fix Tiff's hair and do my best to think of all the little things she would have done had she been able. I would, to the best of my ability, try to get into Debbie's heart and mind and leave no stone unturned. I would try to remember every detail to share with her.

I left her that night feeling that my heart would break.

Before I went to bed I looked over our mail. I checked the obituary in the Huntsville Times.

The first person listed was Tiffany Leigh Stinson, three years old. "She died Tuesday at a Birmingham hospital. The funeral will be Friday at 10 a.m. at Whitesburg Baptist Church. Burial will be in Valhalla Memory Gardens."

> So matter of fact.
> So cold.
> So real.
> So unchangeable.
> But not final!

We will bury your body, Tiff. But we will not say, "Goodbye." We will be together again, forever together because of Jesus. Nothing cold about that!

And, oh, so real!

That truth is unchangeable.

No more death! No more separation! No more tears! No more sickness!

> "Oh, death, where is your victory? Oh, death, where is your sting? Thanks be to God, who gives us the victory through our Lord Jesus Christ". I Corinthians 15:56 nas

I fell asleep, exhausted, but at peace.

3. *Temporary Goodbye*

Thursday morning began a most difficult day. My dear friend, Brenda, drove us to all our appointments.

The funeral home was first. Arrangements were made and casket selected. Then we went into the room where Tiffany's body lay.

Her hair was washed and looked and felt like spun gold. Her face was so beautiful - not like a corpse. It was like a master artist had painted shadows and highlights, creating a magnificent work of art. Surely God's angels had guided someone's hands.

Barbara put her dress on.

I said, "Okay, Tiff, one last time we'll blow your beautiful hair dry. There had been so many times I had watched her at my vanity saying, "I dry my hair." How prissy she was! With the help of a curling iron, I made soft curls to lie on the white pillow. Her pretty lacy bow with ribbon streamers was put in her hair. It was pink, of course. She looked like a real doll. The thought went through my mind that someone needed to use her as a model for a Precious Moments doll.

There was a very nice man who stayed in the room with

us. He didn't understand how I was doing this. I asked him if he knew Jesus Christ personally. He said, "No." I urged him to reach out to Jesus! That's the only way I know that anyone could get through this kind of emotionally draining tragedy.

We went from the funeral home to Valhalla Memory Gardens to sign some papers there. A nice young man met with us. He knew all about our circumstances and was so sympathetic. I asked him if he had children. He said, "Yes." I begged him to be sure he kept his priorities in order. Life is so uncertain. Make sure you lead your family to walk with the Lord daily in order that you are all prepared if and when a crisis comes your way.

Next stop was Albert's Florist. Tiffany loved pink. I wanted an airy casket spray with lots of baby's breath, pink sweetheart roses and so on.

There were no pink sweetheart roses to be found in Huntsville. Albert took an interest in this himself. As I tried to explain my desires for this to be special, I began to cry. I told him about our little precious three year old angel. He assured me that he would fix the spray himself, and that it would be beautiful. And it was!

Thursday night was a visitation time at the funeral home. Friends were staying with Debbie. She had been moved into a private room at this point, much sooner than the doctors had anticipated.

A flood of friends and family came by to comfort us. So many of them had the unusual sense that there was something special about Tiffany's body. It didn't look like the dead bodies we had seen before.

Skip shared that he had feared looking at her body because he didn't think he could bear seeing her with that look of death. He was so relieved to see how beautiful her body looked. I believe God touched her little body in an unusual way for Skip's sake.

The service on Friday was everything, and so much more, than I had hoped for. Tim Thomassian and Doug Seaver led all of us as we sang *In This Very Room* at the beginning. I felt such a peace as I paid close attention to the words.

In this very room there's quite enough love for one like me, and in this very room there's quite enough joy for one like me, and there's quite enough hope and quite enough power to chase away any gloom, for Jesus, Lord Jesus is in this very room. And in this very room there's quite enough love for all of us. And in this very room there's quite enough joy for all of us, and there's quite enough hope and quite enough power to chase away any gloom, for Jesus, Lord Jesus is in this very room. And in this very room there's quite enough love for all the world. And in this very room there's quite enough joy for all the world. And there's quite enough joy and quite enough power to chase away any gloom, for Jesus, Lord Jesus is in this very room.

Then Doug sang *Jesus Loves Me,* which was Tiffany's favorite song.

Brother Herman shared his lovely memories of Tiffany. Skip and Debbie had joined his church when Tiffany was a little baby.

He read a letter from two of Tiffany's Sunday school teachers.

Dear Brother Herman,

I hope these few pleasant thoughts of Tiffany will make your difficult job a little easier.

As a first time teacher of two and three-year-olds, I was a little apprehensive of my abilities to teach such a young group. My fears vanished when a little blond with big eyes crawled into my lap and asked, "What is our Jesus story about?" Tiffany made me feel very welcomed.

Tiffany was always a good mother to our Sunday school dolls. She would wrap them in blankets and stroll them around the room in a small plastic grocery cart. Most of all, her favorite item was a pair of pink ladies high-heel shoes. Every Sunday, Tiffany would make a "bee" line for the toy box, dig out the heels, take off her own shoes and replace them with the heels.

During our story time, Tiffany would make room in our circle for her buggy full of dolls. She would sit in her chair, cross her little legs with those big pink shoes on, and listen intently to our "Jesus" story. Memories of Tiffany will always bring a smile.

Our prayers are also with you, Brother Herman.

In God's Love,

Susie & Mable

Then he read a poem he had written after Tiffany died.

> *Pink Shoes and Heaven*
> *Sunday morning was the scene*
> *Walking the walk at the church,*
> *A beautiful little thing,*
> *All dressed in pink frills*
> *Caused this pastor's heart a thrill.*
> *A tiny white purse and Testament in hand*

Would make any Daddy proud to be her man.

To the classroom, she'd stroll
Straight for a toy box, she'd go.
An old pair of high heels, she'd put on
In her mind, a lady all grown.

Now in Heaven, down streets she strolls,
Along with Jesus His hand she holds.
"There is no reason to fear," she says;
"Because you too can come here."
It is Sunday morning in Heaven every day
Be assured Tiffany is at play.

Herman Pair,
Tiffany's Pastor

Brother Jimmy, our pastor at Whitesburg Baptist Church, had the message. You could tell his heart was broken, too. His words were evangelistic in their thrust, but so personal and such a comfort. I remember when he looked at Skip and said, "Skip, I know how you must be hurting right now. I want to tell you your little girl is not out there somewhere alone. She's in the safest place she could be. She's in the loving care of Jesus. She will never be separated from Him. He's taking care of your little girl."

What a comfort that truth is to all of us!

While we were having our service in Huntsville, there was a little service going on in Debbie's room. Brother Dick Thomassian, our Minister of Music who had meant so much to Debbie as a teenager, got Jeff Flinn, the Chaplain at Carraway, and a few others, and they sang the same songs that we heard. Brother

Dick shared a sweet message that brought such precious comfort to Debbie's soul.

Before the day ended, we all were praising our God for once again ministering to us in such a special way.

I was physically exhausted that evening, but with much persuasion; I talked everyone into letting me spend that special night with Debbie.

We shared our deep feelings in our mother/daughter quiet time. What solid bonding takes place in moments like those.

Debbie finally went to sleep. I'll never forget that night. Curled up in that uncomfortable chair, as cold as an ice cube, I was unable to sleep.

I just looked at Debbie and was so grateful that she and Garrett were alive, and that we didn't have to bury three of our babies. I thanked God over and over for His grace and His mercy.

I was thinking about all the casts on her arms and leg and at the way her beautiful face was cut up. I was sick thinking of the pain she must have experienced physically as they tore her flesh and pulled on those broken limbs as they freed her from that demolished car.

The words to a song in *Celebrate Life* started going through my mind. It was Mary speaking as they took her Son from the cross, broken and bleeding.

"Carry Him gently, my baby. Carry Him gently my child.
Carry Him far from suffering.
Let Him rest, let Him rest for awhile."

I thought, "Oh, God, were they gentle with my baby? Did they realize how special she was? I began to cry uncontrollably.

Through my tears, I watched Debbie as she slept. I finally dozed off from sheer exhaustion.

Laddie kept a constant vigil in Debbie's room. His sweet, tender, gentle, fatherly love for his daughter won the hearts of all those who came in to care for Debbie.

One of the very special moments when God used some-one to touch Debbie in an unusual way was when Jimmie Ruth Caughron sang for her. The song was *"He'll Find a Way,"* written by Babbie Mason.

At times the load is heavy
At times the road is long
When circumstances come your way
And you think you can't go on
When you're feeling at your weakest
Jesus will be strong
He'll provide an answer
When you think all hope is gone
He'll find a way.

For I know that if He can paint a sunset
Put the stars in place
I know that if He can raise up mountains
And calm the storm tossed waves
And if He can conquer death forever
And open Heaven's gates
I know for you
He'll see you though
He'll find a way.

And at times your heart is breaking
With a pain that's so intense

And all you hold are broken pieces
To a life that makes no sense
He wants to lift you up and hold you
And mend each torn event
He'll pick up the pieces
That you thought had all been spent.
He'll find a way.

For I know that if He can paint a sunset
Put the stars in place
I know that if He can raise up mountains
And calm the storm tossed waves
And if He can conquer death forever
And open Heaven's gates
I know for you
He'll see you though
He'll find a way.
He'll find a way.

Those in the room were weeping. Debbie listened intently with that peace on her countenance that defied explanation. Only the presence and power of the Holy Spirit of God Himself could make her shine so beautifully from within. She said softly, "Thank you, J.R. Now, I think I'll rest awhile."

4. *Garrett's Adjustment*

It was Saturday. The good news was that Garrett was going to be released from the hospital. He had gotten so much attention and so many presents that, by the end of his stay, he was enjoying himself very much.

He walked with a slight limp because of his little fracture in one hip. His cut was healing very nicely. He lost one tooth in the accident. All of us felt so sorry for him that we pitched in on behalf of the tooth fairy, and he got twenty-eight dollars. He was ready to pull the rest of his teeth and get enough money to buy all the Nintendo games he wanted.

Skip and I took him by to see Debbie before we took him home.

He was shocked to see his mother's face, and as only a child can, he blurted out, "Mommy, you look horrible!"

Observing his cuts, bruises and black eyes, she said, "You don't look so great yourself."

He curled up in a chair and went to sleep.

When we got Garrett home, he went into a depression that

was frightening to me. It was as though an invisible wall went up that separated him from everyone except his daddy.

The afternoon we brought Garrett home from the hospital, I noticed that Skip seemed to be unusually quiet. He would go into the house and in a few minutes would hurry back outdoors. One of these times, he stayed for more than an hour. He did not want anything to eat. Something was obviously very wrong.

I hesitated to intrude on his private pain and thought he might need to be by himself. But finally, I began to think that maybe he needed someone to talk to. I went out and sat down on the steps by him and asked if he would like to talk.

He told me that he just couldn't stand going into the house. Everywhere he looked, he saw her handprints on the walls or other memories of Tiffany. It was just more than he could handle. He went on to tell me that when he looked up into the sky, he couldn't see or understand beyond the trees. He knew that Tiffany was with God in heaven, but heaven seemed so far away.

He wanted more than anything at that moment to be with Tiffany, wherever she was. The pain and emotional suffering I saw in his eyes tore my heart out. I wanted so desperately to be able to do something to comfort him.

I remember saying to him, "Tiffany doesn't need you now. She is in the care of Jesus. But there is a little five-year-old son inside that house who needs a father, and not just any father; he needs a godly father. And you have a wife lying in that hospital who is suffering mentally and emotionally and physically. She needs a strong support system more than she ever has in her whole life. She needs you to be there for her for many months to come."

I went on, with a river of tears falling out of my brokenness, to explain to him that we understood his pain. We were devastated over our only little granddaughter's death. We had so looked forward to seeing all our hopes and dreams for her come to pass in the land of the living. But we were hurting even more for our baby, who was not only struggling to survive physically, but was denied the privilege of being with her baby those final hours. She did not get to hold her beautiful little body and say good-bye to her. But you see, what they were feeling for their three-year-old baby was the exact same pain we were feeling for our thirty-three year old baby. It doesn't matter how old they are, they are always your baby.

The time of sharing seemed to clear up some things that needed to be verbalized. We got up. Skip hugged me real tight. We went inside. He said, "I feel real hungry now." In the refrigerator, waiting for him, was a big hoagie sandwich that someone had brought for him. He popped it into the microwave, chowed down, and was able to go into the den, recline in his chair, and watch television.

Several days went by. One day, I asked Garrett if he would like to have a special friend come over to play with him. He said he wanted Richard Victor Collins, III to come over. I got the telephone book down and hurriedly searched for Richard Victor Collins, II. His Mother brought him over, and the invisible wall was gone.

I listened to the two of them talking about Tiffany and Heaven and Jesus and even the Devil. They agreed that they would circle Jesus because Jesus was good, and X the Devil because he was evil. They ran in to tell me this personally.

Garrett said, "Ree, does Tiffany have a swimming pool in Heaven?" I told him I didn't know about a pool, but I did know there are rivers in Heaven, and they are good places to swim.

Garrett asked Richard if he went to Sunday school. Richard said he did sometimes, but mostly they just read Bible stories at home.

Garrett said, "Ree, reading Bible stories at home isn't as good as going to church, is it?"

Feeling a little like Solomon, I told them that it's best to do both.

They went on to tell each other how they wished their Daddies would go to church with them.

I assured Garrett that his Daddy would be taking him to church when everyone got well. How I wish I could have given Richard the same assurance.

From this visit on, Garrett talked freely about Tiffany. One day, he asked if she could have second helpings of food in Heaven. We all knew that she had a healthy appetite on earth. He said, "We should have put a note in her pocket. Then when the wind blew her dress, it would make the paper rattle. Jesus would hear it, pull the note out and read that Tiffany has permission to have second helpings."

One evening, Garrett and I were out looking for lightning bugs. When we passed Blackie's doghouse, Garrett told me that he and Tiff had played a lot of times in the doghouse. I commented that I knew he must really miss her. He got upset and said, "Everybody always says that. They always say, 'I know you miss her.'"

"What do you think we should say?" I asked.

He thought awhile and said, "Just I wish she could come back down here for a little while. She's not coming back, and she didn't even take her toys with her."

Garrett, on several occasions, went into great detail about Tiffany's resurrected body. One day, he said if she could come back for a visit, and if he tried to follow her around, she could go through a wall and he would run right into it.

About two weeks before the accident, Debbie called me and asked if I would try and calm Tiffany down. She and the children were talking about going to Heaven when you died. Tiff asked if Papa and Ree were going to die and go to Heaven. Debbie said, "Yes," and commented on how happy they were that they would know that for sure.

Both Tiffany and Garrett began to cry. Tiff was saying over and over, "I don't want Papa and Ree to die and go to Heaven!"

Debbie put Tiff on the phone.

"Hey, Ree!" she said.

"What's wrong, Baby," I asked.

"Ree, are you and Papa going to die and go to Heaven?"

"Not right away, Sweetheart. I think we'll wait a few years and watch you grow up and get married and have babies!" I replied.

"Oh, well, would you buy me some more presents?" she asked, with a sign of relief.

Somehow, I realized that much of her concern was that she might lose her proverbial Santa Claus.

5. *The Wreck*

At different times, Debbie told Laddie and me about God preparing her for this tragedy. The morning of the accident, she was in the kitchen. A strong impression in her spirit conveyed to her that there would be a crisis. She was not to be afraid, because she would not die.

She tried to shake it off. That afternoon, she and Tiff buckled up and went to pick up Garrett at kindergarten. After he got into the back seat and buckled up, which was something Debbie always insisted on, they headed for the grocery store.

There was a sudden rainstorm. After many weeks of drought, the road was slick.

A sixteen-year-old boy in a pickup truck was leaving school to go home. He had gotten his driver's license two weeks earlier.

Witnesses saw him pull over into Debbie's lane, and he hit them head on. These witnesses testified that Debbie was going less than the speed limit and driving down the center of her lane.

Debbie saw black and did not see the truck hit them. The car folded on her side. Two vertebrae snapped in Tiffany's neck. They controlled her heart and her breathing. She was brain dead immediately. Paramedics were able to start her heart beating and put her on a machine. I believe in my heart that her little spirit was with her Jesus immediately.

The brake pedal and the clutch were pushed up and crushed Debbie's heel, broke her ankle and crushed her kneecap.

The steering wheel was shoved into her chest, bruising her breasts and puncturing a lung that later collapsed. Her left arm took a powerful blow that shattered her elbow and damaged many nerves down the arm, resulting in no sensation in her fingers.

The hood came through the windshield and scalped her forehead. Her nose looked like someone had pounded it with a meat cleaver. Glass had stuck in her eyes and hair and everywhere. Laddie was picking bits of glass out of her body for weeks.

As she was pinned in, unable to move at all and unable to see as her glasses were shattered, she heard Garrett cry.

She told him to be calm and to look out the windows and see all the people who were there to help them. He passed out, obviously unable to handle such a trauma.

Debbie did not hear Tiffany crying. She knew instinctively that the impression she had that morning was God preparing her for this. She was not afraid that she would die. God had told her *she* would not. It was Tiffany who would die.

This explained why she kept asking from the minute we saw her, "Is Tiffany okay? Is Tiffany dead?"

Debbie has recall of almost everything from the accident to the hospital and through the Intensive Care experience.

As all the people ministered to her through the following days, she was the one who continuously amazed everyone with her steadfast courage and her positive mental attitude. She had absolute confidence in her God who was too loving to be mean and too wise to make a mistake. Laddie and I rejoiced over the depth of her faith. She taught us so much about how to trust God in the midst of one of life's most difficult and heartbreaking crises. We have always been proud of our daughter, but never more so than during this time.

Debbie's mental, emotional and spiritual attitude caused her healing process to accelerate.

She was out of Intensive Care in three days and out of the hospital in ten days.

We were told that she would be in a wheelchair for three months and then maybe she could get around with a walking cast. This would stay on another six weeks at least. Whether or not the heel would stay together when she stood on it was the concern.

By the three-month appointment, she was walking without a cast of any kind.

Laddie and I, for all intents and purposes, moved to Birmingham for the summer. We would come back to our home on the weekend so that we could teach our Sunday school class.

We did this until Debbie was able to walk by herself. We were glad to get back home, but even more thankful for the way God was healing her body so miraculously.

One of the things that I believe helped a lot was that she had no hatred toward the young boy. None of us did.

A couple of weeks after the accident, Skip stopped by the service station where the boy's father worked. He told him that he wanted him to know that he wasn't sitting around his house hating his son. He explained that he had to believe that this was a part of a greater plan that God had, even though he didn't understand it all.

We realized that there was not enough strength left after we got through a day's workload to expend any energy on a negative emotion like hatred or bitterness.

Only God could have accomplished this and given us the victory in this area. How we do praise Him for that!

6. *A Letter to Tiffany*

Dear Tiff,

It's been such a long time since you came to Papa/Ree's the last time. We've missed you so much since you went to live with Jesus.

I always thought we would be the ones who left first and waited for you. But as it turned out, you were the privileged one.

Your Mommy and Daddy and your Papa/Ree wanted the very best for you and Garrett. Even though we have experienced such a void in our lives without you, we know without a doubt that you do have the very best now and forever.

I've thought so many times about how excited your grandmother Mary, your great grandparents, and Wilbur must have been when Jesus gathered you in His arms and took you to them.

You must have lit up Heaven when you prissed up and down those streets of gold.

I've thought so many times about your last Mother's Day visit. I can see you now when we got to church that morning. You were all dressed up with your white patent shoulder strap purse on your arm, carrying your two New Testaments, two Certs and your offering for Jesus.

"I go to Sunny school *by myself,*" you said with such authority.

Your Mother and I watched you go around the corners of the corridors; your little behind just prissing back and forth. When you got to your room, you stopped and knocked, just like the sign on the door said.

The door opened, and Mr. and Mrs. Demirjian, your favorite teachers, saw you come in.

"There's Tiffany! I told you she'd be here today!"

Mr. Demirjian told us that his wife got up that morning and said, "It's Mother's Day. I'll bet Tiffany will be here today."

You were and are so special to everyone who ever met you.

You made a beautiful gift for your mother that day. It was a flower to go in a shadow box frame. The day of your Memorial Service, Mrs. Collier gave it to me to give to your mommy. They had kept it all that time. Your mommy will treasure it because you made it.

Every time I got in the swimming pool this summer, I thought of you. Garrett asked me if you would have a pool in Heaven.

We loved to watch you swim. Remember how you used to float on your back and spew water out like a baby whale?

Tiff, one of my favorite memories is of you and Garrett doing your "Presentings" by the pool. Garrett would do his raisin man imitation. You would dance and sing, "And He Say." The only thing is, you left before you told us what "he say."

Aunt Jane was telling me about how she remembers when you curled up in her lap in the rocking chair and let her rock you and love on you.

Aunt Barbara's favorite memory was the Christmas your baby doll wouldn't fit in the buggy, and you used brute force to squash her in. We all had a good laugh when you got into the buggy and over went buggy, Tiffy and all. You didn't care! You just got up and went to the next toy.

One of my all time favorite memories is of you at Papa/Ree's thirty-fifth wedding anniversary party your Mama gave for us.

Everything was so beautiful on the dining room table. You got your plate, just like the adults, and went around the table reaching up and taking whatever your little fingers could reach. You were too short to see.

You got six cups of punch and lined them up on the island in the kitchen. Then you brought your plate down to the den, climbed up in the chair by me, crossed your legs and ate your goodies. Then back to the table to get another plate and start all over again. You were so adorable!

Tiff, I still put candy in the dish on the coffee table. It just doesn't get eaten much anymore. No one seems to want to check it out. The first place you went when you came to visit was to the candy dish. Then you went to Papa's closet to check out what he had left on his chest. You usually found Certs and Rolaids and money and who knows what else. Fortunately, you always rejected the Rolaids. Then it was over to my closet to get high heel shoes, and then to my vanity to blow your hair dry and put on a little makeup and some jewelry.

Your femininity was such a delight to your Mommy and Ree. Your Mommy always had you dressed so pretty and had your fingernails polished. She put hot rollers in your hair and fluffed it out and put those precious little hair ornaments and bows in your beautiful blonde hair. You would swirl around like a little model.

I got such a joy out of buying or making you something special. I've wanted so badly to make you a little "buttons and bows" sweatshirt this fall. Miss Dana had made some for her girls. You would have loved the pretty bright colors.

I know these colors here are so dull in comparison to the brightness of Heaven.

I was thinking about you one day, and I remembered something I had taught in Jeremiah 1:5. God said, "Before I formed you in the womb, I knew you; before you were born, I sanctified you."

I believe with all my heart that God had something so extra special in mind when He made you, my sweet Tiff.

You brought so much joy into all our lives. Your short three years created enough sweet memories to last a lifetime. Your physical death has touched the hearts and spirits of thousands of people across the country. I believe God accomplished all that He had in mind when He created and sanctified you. *"Behold, children are a gift of the Lord...."* Psalm 127:3 (NAS)

When your Mommy was a little girl, I worried so that she might get sick and die. One day, I read a little book, *Dearest Debbie.* It was a letter Dale Evans Rogers wrote to her daughter who was killed in a bus accident. I believe someone sent her a copy of this poem. When I read the poem, it helped me so much to overcome my fear of losing my child in death.

> "I'll lend you for a little while,
> a child of Mine," He said,
> "For you to love the while she lives,
> And mourn when she is dead.
> It may be six or seven years,
> or twenty-two or three,
> But will you, till I call her back,
> take care of her for Me?
> She'll bring her charms to gladden you,

and tho' her stay be brief,
You will have lovely memories
as solace for your grief.

"I cannot promise she will stay,
since all from earth return,
But there are lessons taught down here
I want this child to learn.
I have looked the world-wide over
in my search for teachers true,
And from the throngs that crowd life's lanes,
I have selected you.
Now will you give her all your love,
nor think the labor vain,
Nor hate Me when I come to call
to take her back again?

We fancied that we heard them say,
"Dear Lord, Thy will be done!
For all the joy Thy child will bring,
the risk of grief we run.
We will shelter her with tenderness,
we will love her while we may,
And for the happiness we have now,
forever grateful stay.
But shall the angels call for her
much sooner than we planned,
We shall brave the bitter grief that comes
and try to understand."

I understand the poem better now. We are so thankful that
God chose to entrust you to our family. We cannot be anything

but grateful for the joy of caring for you, loving you and being loved by you.

Our hope is that we taught you well. We know we loved you deeply. You were our "bet priend." (Tiffany's pronunciation of "best friend.")

Mommy, Daddy, Garrett and Papa/Ree love you and miss you so much. Until Jesus comes, or until I die, I will remember you with a smile and probably a tear or two.

Ree

P.S. Tiff, we knew the first Christmas without you would be sad. Sure enough, we reluctantly pulled out the Christmas tree and trimmings. Papa was putting the artificial tree together. I pulled out a bundle wrapped in tissue paper. When I opened it, I saw those beautiful stockings your Mommy made for you and Garrett. Garrett's name was perfect. Your name was done in red sequins. Half of them were missing. Tiffany was not on the stocking. Tiffany was not here.

I missed you terribly. I cried so hard. I didn't know what to do about hanging your stocking. Papa said I shouldn't. But something made me put both of the gray mouse hangers on the mantle. I hung Garrett's, and then I hung yours. Oh, how I cried!

The next day, I took your stocking down. I put a new ornament on the tree and wrote your name in gold with Christmas, 1988, on it. I had worked through another part of my pain. We're going to put a specially chosen new ornament on each year in your memory. We also placed a poinsettia in the church in your memory.

As much as we missed you, we rejoiced knowing this was, indeed, your best Christmas ever—right there in the very presence of the Christ of Christmas!

Rejoice, and again I say, rejoice!

7. *Lessons Learned*

A greater tragedy than the accident would be if we, having gone through such a severe trial, came out of it exactly as we were before, having learned little.

With a grateful and singing heart, I praise God that this did not happen to our family.

So many eyes were on us to see whether or not the scriptural truths we had taught would, indeed, work.

I could not write about the crisis and its consequences without sharing with the reader the lessons learned as a result of these unexpected visitors.

The suddenness of an automobile accident, a death, a spouse who walks in one day and announces they have fallen in love with someone else and they do not love you anymore, a house that burns down or a tornado from nowhere blows to kingdom come treasures of yours that have so many beautiful memories—these give you no time to prepare yourself mentally, emotionally and spiritually. Panic sets in as all the negative thoughts flood your mind, telling you just how impossible it will be for you to cope.

None of us knows when we get up on any given day what we will face before its twenty-four hours pass.

It takes months and years of being a disciplined student of God's word to be able when the crisis comes to have His Word pour from within you, speaking peace and giving instruction and direction each step of the way.

It does not just drop on you by a process of osmosis. As many have inquired as to how we walked through this trial with faith and confidence and even in joy, they have expressed that it frightens them because they know they could not do the same.

My advice is, instead of being a defeatist, find out what worked and commit yourself to developing discipline in that area of your own life.

God does not pick and choose one of us over another to be strong or courageous. This is what He expects from all His soldiers of the cross. In our flesh, we can do nothing. In Christ, we can do all things! Which do you choose?

The Bible says:

"Be strong, in the Lord, and in the strength of His might.

Put on the whole armor of God, that you may be able to stand firm against the schemes of the devil.

For our struggle is not against flesh and blood, but against the rulers, against the powers, against the world forces of this darkness, against the spiritual forces of wickedness in heavenly places.

Therefore, take up the full armor of God that you may be able to resist in the evil day, and having done everything, to stand firm.

Stand firm, therefore, having girded your loins with truth, and having put on the breastplate of righteousness, and having shod your feet with the preparation of the Gospel of Peace.

In addition to all, taking up the shield of faith with which you will be able to extinguish all the flaming missiles of the evil one.

And take the helmet of salvation, and the sword of the Spirit, which is the word of God.

With all prayer and petition, pray at all times in the Spirit, and with this in view, be on the alert with all perseverance and petition for all the saints." Ephesians 6: 10–18. (nas)

It is imperative that each of us realizes the necessity of taking the time to start a day talking to our Father, drawing close to Him, praising Him and putting on our whole armor before we go out to face the day's spiritual warfare.

Satan and his evil workers are always on hand. They take a circumstance that comes our way, and get to work on our minds, weaving a web of confusion and anxiety. Their ultimate goal is to destroy us mentally, emotionally, physically and spiritually. Satan would love to see us join with him against God and God's purpose for us. If he cannot accomplish that, he will work to keep us from surrendering to God's will by keeping us struggling in our own strength, becoming depressed and, hopefully, ultimately taking our lives to get relieved of the struggle.

But God ...yes, but God wants to take that same trial, and He says "Come unto Me." He wants to show us more of Himself than we've ever seen before. He wants to refine us as we go through the fire, burning away that dross that dulls our testimony. Often, a goldsmith takes the gold and puts it through a hammering process, thus producing an especially beautiful transparent gold.

I believe our family, especially Debbie, experienced the "hammering." I am still hearing from people about how they were never the same after seeing how Jesus Christ was shining through Debbie's lacerated face.

That doesn't just happen. The Bible says, *"Train your child in the way they should go."* The Bible says, *"Grow in the grace and knowledge of our Lord and Savior Jesus Christ"* (II Peter 3: 18), *and in wisdom, and stature and in favor with God and man."* (Luke 2: 52)

My aim is to break down the lessons learned into three chapters. First, hide the word of God in your heart daily; second, cultivate the bonds of love among others in the family of God; third, rejoice in the assurance of our eternal dwelling place.

May these thoughts and reflections strengthen your faith and challenge your commitment to our Lord to grow deeper. That is my prayer.

8. *Earthen Vessels Storehouses of God's Treasures*

From the very moment that Jesus Christ, in the person and power of the Holy Spirit, came into my life when I was just thirty years old, I have had an insatiable hunger to know Him better and to feed on His Word.

> "For it is the God who commanded light to shine out of darkness, who has shone in our hearts to give the light of the knowledge of the glory of God in the face of Jesus Christ.

> But we have this treasure in earthen vessels that the excellence of the power may be of God and not of us." II Corinthians 4:6–7

It's true …God did make a light shine out of darkness that day. I had for many years felt my life spinning out of control. And yet it never occurred to me or to anyone else as a matter of fact, that I had a spiritual problem. All the people and things I trusted my soul's security to ultimately proved to be sinking sand.

But Jesus said to me, *"Come unto me, all ye who labor and are heavy laden, and I will give you rest. Take my yoke upon you and learn of me, for I am meek and lowly in heart, and you shall find rest unto your soul, for my yoke is easy and my burden is light".* Matthew 11:28–30

I confessed that day that I had never really prayed. I simply asked Him if He could do something with my mess, and if He could, He could have all of me for the rest of my life. For some unexplainable reason, (except that He demonstrated His love for me while I was yet a sinner by dying for me), He reached down in loving kindness, forgave me my sins—*amazing grace*—and even came into my life to live in me.

I exchanged all that I was—fearful, depressed, self-centered, defeated and the list could go on and on—for all that He is—love, peace, joy, gentle, kind, faithful, controlled, and the list could go on and on. I don't understand it, but like the blind man said, *"I only know, whereas I was blind, now I see."*

Depression left when Jesus entered. I might add that it has not returned. You see, as I began to satisfy my hunger for Jesus with His word, learning more about Him each day as we walked together up that Calvary Road or as I sometimes refer to it, my Heavenly Highway, there was no room there for a mindset that pulled you down.

I have had many circumstances and trials come my way in the past years that would have blown me away before Jesus. But with God, Himself, Creator of the Universe and Redeemer of my soul, living in me in the powerful overcoming presence of His Holy Spirit, and with Jesus Christ, my High Priest, sitting at the right hand of our Father, ever living to make intercession for me, how can I fail to know victory and to be content in spite of circumstances?

It's true..."*Yet in all these things we are more than conquerors through Him who loved us,*" Romans 8:37.

It's true..."*Whoever hears these sayings of Mine, and does them, I will liken him to a wise man who built his house upon the rock; and the rain descended,* the floods came, and the winds blew and beat on that house; and *it did not fall, for it was founded on the rock.*

But everyone who hears these sayings of Mine, and does not do them, will be like a foolish man, who built his house on the sand; and the rain descended, the floods came, and the winds blew and beat on that house, and it fell. And great was its fall," Matthew 7:24–27.

There is no promise given us when we are born again and become a part of God's family that we will be delivered from trials and tribulations. He didn't promise that we might sit in our material comfort looking through our rosy glasses, enjoying perfect health, and turning our noses slightly upward when catching a glimpse of some poor sinner who isn't as holy as we are.

It's true...Jesus said, "*In this world you will have tribulations; but be of good cheer, I have overcome the world,*" John 16:33b.

It's true..."*Therefore, having been justified by faith, we have peace with God through our Lord Jesus Christ, through whom, also, we have access by faith into this grace in which we stand, and, rejoice in hope of the glory of God. And not only that, but we also glory in tribulations, knowing that tribulation produces perseverance; and perseverance, character, and character, hope. Now hope doesn't disappoint, because the love of God has been poured out in our hearts by the Holy Spirit who was given to us,*" Romans 5:1–5.

It's true..."*Blessed be the God and Father of our Lord Jesus Christ, the Father of mercies and God of all comfort, who comforts us in all our tribulation, that we may be able to comfort those who are in any trouble, with the comfort with which we ourselves are comforted by God,"* I Corinthians 1:3–5.

It's true …The bottom line is *"that we should not trust in ourselves, but in God who raises the dead,"* I Corinthians 1:9.

It's true . . ."*Blessed be the God and Father of our Lord Jesus Christ, who according to His abundant mercy has begotten us again to a living hope through the resurrection of Jesus Christ from the dead; to an inheritance incorruptible and undefiled and that does not fade away, reserved in Heaven for you, who are kept by the power of God through faith for salvation ready to be revealed in the last time.*

In this you greatly rejoice, though now for a little while, if need be, you have been grieved by various trials, that the genuineness of our faith, being much more precious than gold that perishes, though it is tested by fire, many be found to praise, honor, and glory at the revelation of Jesus Christ, whom having not seen you love. Though now you do not see Him, yet believing, you rejoice with joy inexpressible and full of glory, receiving the end of your faith - the salvation of your souls," I Peter 1:3–9.

It's true …"*My brethren, count it all joy, when you fall into various trials, knowing that the testing of your faith produces patience. But let patience have its perfect work, that you may be perfect (mature) and complete, lacking nothing. If any of you lacks wisdom, let him ask of God, who gives to all liberally and without reproach, and it will be given to you,"* James 1:2–5.

Why have I laid out so much scripture with an emphasis on the phrase "It's true?"

God has repeatedly stressed the importance of us knowing and doing His word. This is a vital part of the building of our lives upon the Rock. Rains, floods, winds and anything Satan hurls out of Hell at us cannot cause our house to fall. It's built on the Rock.

We stand tall, face toward the storms, trusting in the truth that God is who He says He is, and nothing is too hard for Him. He is all-powerful.

We remember time and again how He has proven that He is love, and it is not in His nature to be mean.

We recall that He has declared that He is all-knowing, the source of true wisdom and it is impossible for Him to make a mistake. We trust in Him with all our hearts and consider it a sane and sound decision to let Him direct our paths.

And so we save much needed strength and energy by not getting angry at God and blaming Him for not doing something to deliver us from our pain or suffering.

These are some things that were settled long before May 23, 1988. Once the commitment has been made to trust God and His word unreservedly, (if God says it, that settles it), you do not have to be fearful of anything or anybody ever again.

I realize, of course, that there is a daily reckoning with the flesh that never gives up the hope that it will somehow find a way to entice us to turn our minds, emotions, and will over to it.

But it's true . . ."*I choose this day whom I will serve. I will serve the Lord,*" Joshua 24:15b.

It's true . . . Jesus said He left me His peace; not an absence of trouble, but a peace in the midst of the storm. The world cannot begin to fathom such a thing.

He said He left me His joy; not a giddy euphoria, but rather, a contented soul, resting in the sanctuary under the shadow of His wings.

He brought into my life His love, agape love, unconditional

love, a love that obeys His command for us to love one another as Christians, but more than that, His love that loves my enemies, too.

What an inheritance! And that's not all of what we were given. But all we were given is all in Jesus! Praise God from whom all blessings flow!

When my earthly father died, he left a will dividing his earthly goods equally between his four children. It was a legal document. One fourth belonged to me. No one could take it from me. I could have said, "I don't need it or want it," and turned around and given to anyone I pleased, or I could have thrown it away so as not to benefit anyone. I chose to receive it for myself, and use it in a way that would have pleased my father.

Now, when Jesus left me the inheritance of peace, love and joy, it was indeed mine by way of grace through faith. No one can take my inheritance from me, but I can give it up to circumstances that are difficult or to people who make me miserable. If I squander it by giving it up and thus becoming a defeated child of God—no peace, love or joy—I trample under foot the blood of Jesus that was shed on Calvary's cross to cover my sins and free me to live a victorious Christian life. I must confess this as sin, repent, reclaim my inheritance (and I can do that), and determine never to be so foolish with God's treasures in my earthen vessel again.

The wise man or woman walks in daily obedience, knowing the importance of loving God with all his heart, clinging to that which is pure and fleeing from that which is evil, being ready in season and out of season to share your testimony as to God's faithfulness.

If it is my choice, and it is, I choose to honor the Giver by treasuring and being a good steward of His gift to me.

This is how we got through the accident and the months that followed.

A severe crisis never leaves you just as you were before it happened. It either drives you far from God, either in ignoring Him or in screaming out your hatred for Him; or it draws you closer to Him than you have ever been.

There are many roads you can go down and ways you can try to dull your mind so you don't have to face the reality of death or some other major trial. You can block it out for awhile, but eventually, you come back to face the inevitable pain again and again. It will go nowhere. It will wait for you to face it head on. Some find this to be more than they can handle and find that suicide looks like the only answer.

But you see . . .

It's true . . ."*It's appointed unto man, to die once, but after this the judgment,*" Hebrews 9:27.

Pulling the trigger or taking the pills was not the end. How much better it would have been had they gone to God with their brokenness and confusion and let Him, who is the friend of a wounded heart, give them comfort and new life and a purpose for the future.

For others, their crisis may do just this; bring them to Jesus Christ for salvation.

For many, like our family, it just never occurred to us to blame God or to leave His abiding awesome presence.

It's true . . ."*Seeing then that we have a great High Priest who has passed through the heavens, Jesus the Son of God, let us hold fast our confession.*

For we do not have a High Priest who cannot sympathize with our weaknesses, but was in all points tempted as we are, yet without sin. Let us, therefore, come boldly to the throne of grace that we may obtain mercy and find grace to help in time of need," Hebrews 4:14–16.

We did not hesitate to receive from Jesus the "Grace package" He had put together to more than adequately meet all our needs.

It's true . . ."*Grace and peace be multiplied to you in the knowledge of God and of Jesus, our Lord, as His divine power has given to us all things that pertain to life (our physical and material needs) and godliness (our spiritual needs), through the knowledge of Him, who called us by glory and virtue,"* I Peter 1:2–3.

It's true . . ."*My God shall supply all our need according to His riches in glory by Christ Jesus,"* Philippians 4:19.

It's true . . ."*I can do all things through Christ who strengthens me,"* Philippians 4:13.

All of us will experience going through the Valley of Sorrow or weeping.

It is our choice as to whether we let it ruin our lives. We can let it consume our minds with its negative aspects, and thus thwarting God's desire to build and strengthen our character and produce through us the light that can draw others to Jesus via the tragedy. Or we can with God's help, dig a well, and let God do the positive work of grace in our lives that creates pools of refreshing water for others to drink from and grow from, ultimately bringing honor and glory to Him who deserves our consistent loving faithfulness.

How can we do any less?

9. *God's Family around Us*

The Word of God hidden in our heart is vital to us. It surfaces to comfort, guide and direct us. However, there is still another way God ministered to us. Through his family—His chosen children—He kissed us, hugged us, wrote us, fed us, cared for us, helped us financially, listened to us, and on and on and on, so much more.

These children were members of different churches but at the same time, members of one body, Christ's body.

> "There was the true light which, coming into the world, enlightens every man. He was in the world, and the world was made through Him, and the world did not know Him. He came to His own, and those who were His own did not receive Him. But as many as received Him to them He gave the right to become children of God, even to those who believe in His name, who were born not of blood nor of the will of the flesh nor of the will of man, but of God. ." .John 1:9–13 (nas)

"I'm so glad I'm a part of the family of God.
I've been washed in the fountain
Cleansed by His blood.
Joint heirs with Jesus
As we travel earth's sod.
I'm a part of the family
The family of God."

I think we sing that many times without realizing what an incredible working of God in our lives brought us to the place where we had this become reality in our experience.

A member of the Woods family, my birth family, I can understand. My mother and father, through an act of love, ultimately produced a little human being they named Rita.

A member of the Coker family; I have no problem comprehending that. I married Laddie Coker. We had a baby girl, Debbie. We were a little family.

But a member of God's family? Now that's a stretch for anyone's mind. God, creator/redeemer of the world, wants *me* to be a child of His? The whole universe belongs to Him by virtue of creation. He spoke the universe into existence. He holds it all together. He had a plan and He works His plan, bringing it all to a climax in spite of man and his sin that has done its best, in concert with Satan, to destroy and thwart God's purpose. At that time, every knee will bow and every tongue confess that Jesus Christ is Lord, to the glory of God the Father. The sad thing is these people will have missed out on the joy of being a part of the family of God in this life on earth.

As a result of our placing our faith in Jesus Christ, God adopts us into His family. You don't understand it, but you joyfully accept it as reality, because God said it was so. And your personal experience bears this truth out. God cannot lie!

While we are talking about family, let's take a little time and discuss a part of family life that may help some individual member out. As in any family, the spiritual family members often find themselves caught up in misunderstandings and even hurt feelings.

Our Heavenly Father knows we will experience this because His family is made up of imperfect children, still struggling to overcome their selfish sin nature. One day, when we are delivered from this world either by death or the Rapture, we will be completely free from the bondage of the flesh, but in the meantime, we fight the battle daily of the flesh versus the Spirit. And so, as problems with our spiritual siblings arise, we go to God's Word, and He tells us how to deal with them.

> "Be angry, and yet do not sin; do not let the sun go down
> on your anger, and do not give the devil an opportunity."
> Ephesians 4:26 (nas)

When there is a problem, deal with it immediately. Sit down with your brother or sister, and speaking the truth in love, lay it all out on the table. With scripture as your guide, communicate by giving each person the opportunity to speak and the privilege of being listened to. The Holy Spirit within each of you will lead you into peace, and love will heal any hurts and break down any barriers. Satan will have been defeated, gaining not one inch of ground. Our Father will receive glory, and our testimony will shine, affecting many who are bound by deep roots of bitterness.

> "Let all bitterness and wrath and anger and clamor and
> slander be put away from you, along with all malice,

and be ye kind one to another, tender hearted, forgiving each other, just as God in Christ, also, has forgiven you." Ephesians 4:31–32 (nas)

Bonded together in love, we are sensitive to those around us.

"If one member suffers, all the members suffer with it; if one member is honored, all the members rejoice with it." I Corinthians 12:26 (nas)

It is at this point that I want to share with you how crucial the ministry of the family of God was to our family during the days following the accident.

God had placed one of His children at each place where we would need a special touch from Him. He had the precious lady I told about earlier driving immediately behind Debbie. She was very poised, a quick thinker, a sensitive spirit, a bright and articulate manager of a nursing home with a gift of organization. At the scene of the accident, she went immediately to Debbie, touching her to let her know she was not alone.

When an officer at the scene suggested they just get Debbie and the children to hospitals and then call Skip and tell him about it, this lady said, "No!" She could not bear the thought of Debbie being in that trauma center alone, with her children in another hospital, not knowing whether they were alive or dead. Looking through Debbie's wallet, they could not find a work telephone number. This dear lady thought to look at her checkbook, call the bank, have them look up the account, and bingo, there was a work number. Skip was notified and was there for Debbie before she went into surgery. He then was taken to Children's Hospital to be with Garrett and Tiffany. Very soon he was surrounded by loving friends and members of his spiritual family at Remlap Baptist Church, by neighbors, and as soon as they could get there, his earthly family.

When Laddie and I arrived at Caraway Hospital, God had a chaplain waiting for us. Not just any chaplain though. It was sweet Jeff Flinn who we had known and loved for years. What comfort we felt as he hugged us, and with compassion told us the truth about how bad things looked for our precious babies. We had not even suspected that we would hear our little Tiffany was brain dead. Our hearts sank. But God held us tightly, using Jeff's strong arms.

We went to Children's Hospital. We found Skip, so broken and grieved over the prognosis that Tiffany was leaving. He loved her so, and this simply did not seem possible to be told she was going to die before she had a chance to even begin to grow up. We all had such excitement about her potential for turning the world upside down with her energetic, effervescent personality.

Among those God brought to us at that time, aside from family and local friends, was this lovely lady at the scene of the accident. She introduced herself to us. She said that she told her husband that she could not go to sleep that night until she got to the hospital to tell us that Debbie was not at fault. She was driving perfectly, at the right speed. They were in seat belts. The young boy in the pickup truck crossed the double yellow line and hit them head on. She could not have avoided the accident.

She told us that she had given all the details to the deputies and had a crystal clear memory of all the details and would be available at any time to give this testimony.

She told me she had a little granddaughter about Tiffany's age. "I will never get the image of that beautiful little girl's lifeless body out of my mind the longest day I live," she said to me with tears flowing.

We held each other as I thanked her over and over again for being available to God to be His angel of mercy at this particular time. What a comfort she was to us. When she told me of her relationship to Jesus Christ and her loving commitment to Him, I saw again how blessed we were to have a Father who has a child in the right place so He can use them to touch Debbie, to get in touch with Skip, and to dispel any worry we might have had about what actually had happened.

Two couples who were a part of our spiritual family in Huntsville drove down to be with us. The Calverts and the Karrs stayed with us until the following morning. They were representative of our church family, loving on us physically while the others prayed for God to sustain us with His all sufficient grace. He did indeed answer their prayers.

During the critical period, while we were waiting out the anxious hours in the Intensive Care Unit's family room, we found ourselves in the midst of ministry. Each family in this place awaited news about someone they loved. Hopefully, a doctor would call for them to tell them their parent or child or sibling was out of danger and would soon be moved to a private room. The reality of the situation was that they might be summoned to the conference room to be told that their loved one had died.

As they observed the outpouring of love and kindness shown to us by friends and family, it opened one door after the other for us to share with individuals and with families that this is indeed the way God cares for his children when they are in need. We were able to share food for their physical hunger, but more important than that, we were able to share the Christ, who had declared, "The Spirit of the Lord is upon me because He hath anointed me to preach the gospel to the poor, He had sent me to heal the broken-hearted, to preach deliverance to the captives, and recovering of sight to the blind, to set at liberty them that are bruised, to preach the acceptable year of the Lord" (Luke 4:18–19) This was Jesus' earthly ministry. As a member of Jesus' body, we continue that ministry in His strength.

I had never been in a place where I felt the need for the presence of the Lord more. You could gather together the most educated and skilled physicians and surgeons. You could call for the most spiritual clergymen. You could round up the wisest counselors. But none of them could heal even one of these broken hearts. Bones could mend and scars could heal, but a broken heart remains until Jesus Christ makes it whole again.

I'll never forget the day a young woman came to my sister Barbara and me and asked if we would go to the chapel and pray for her mother. This lady died a few weeks later, but God did a beautiful work in her families' lives preparing them for her physical absence from them. The following Christmas, I got a precious Christmas card from one of the family members thanking us for the way we showed them how to keep your focus on Jesus, knowing, always that He is too loving to be mean and too wise to make a mistake.

Another day, a lovely lady came over to me and asked if I was Rita Coker. She said she had heard me share my Christian testimony several years earlier and that she had remembered my telling about how God had delivered me from depression by way of a born again salvation experience. She told me how impressed she had been with the joy I exuded that day as I talked about the Lord Jesus Christ. She said she had watched me for a couple of days, knowing the circumstances of our tragedy, and had seen for herself that what I had spoken with my lips was reality in my life.

Miraculously, God had protected Debbie from infection, and the word came that she would be moved to a private room after four days. We continued to keep in touch with the other families we had bonded with through those painful days.

Debbie's room was filled with beautiful flowers, baskets of fruit and other goodies, balloons, gifts and cards. Garrett's room was just as full of these things, plus enough toys to make all the children in his wing happy.

Earlier in this book, I told about Brother Dick Thomassian getting together a few choice people and having a memorial service in Debbie's room at the same time we were having Tiffany's service in Huntsville. Friends with all the different gifts of the Holy Spirit came to visit her as they were led by the Spirit.

As previously described in this book, one of the visits was from Jimmie Ruth Caughron. According to her account, she shared with Debbie that a song kept going over and over in her heart as she was driving to the hospital. Debbie asked her to sing it to her. J. R. thought to herself that it would be impossible to get through it when her heart was breaking for Debbie. She went on to say that when she looked across the room at Laddie, his eyes were crying out to her not to disappoint Debbie. And so she sang, "*He'll find a way.*"

This wonderful gift of encouragement came to minister to us in many different ways—the song, the sermons, the service deeds and, many times, through written words. I've chosen a few excerpts or enclosures from some of the letters we received.

One friend wrote, "I ran across a special little verse yesterday in my quiet time that I just had to share with you. It's from Matthew 18:10b, and says, 'the little children's angels do always behold the face of my Father which is in Heaven.' I could just picture that precious little Tiffany sitting in God's lap with His face in her little hands." She also added, "Yesterday, I heard a really neat quote about faith on WNDA. 'Faith is knowing that God is in control …when everything is out of control.'"

Another friend sent us a copy of something that had been found in a Christian Hymn Book, published in 1864, entitled *Death of a Child*:

> *She was the music of our home,*
> *A day that knew no night,*
> *The fragrance of our garden bower,*
> *A thing all smiles and light.*
>
> *Above the couch we bent and prayed*
> *In the half-lighted room,*
> *As the bright hues of infant life*
> *Sank slowly into gloom.*
>
> *The form remained; but there was now*
> *No soul our love to share;*
> *Farewell, with weeping hearts we said,*
> *Child of our love and care.*
>
> *But years are moving quickly past,*
> *And time will soon be o'er;*
> *Death shall be swallowed up in life*
> *On the immortal shore.*
>
> *Then shall we clasp that hand once more,*
> *And smooth that golden hair;*
> *Then shall we kiss those lips again,*
> *When we shall meet her there.*
>
> (Number 1122 by Bonar)

I do not know who to give the credit to for this next enclosure I would like to share with you. All I know is that it is one of those broken hearts that was healed by Jesus. And so I share it, giving the credit to Him.

A sparrow fell, and no one heard. No body cared. It was just a bird. From all the numberless flitting throng of sparrows, who would miss one song? But God leaned down and whispered, "I care, 'twas one of My sparrows, and I was there."

A little girl, all sunshine and laughter, (and sometimes scolding, with kisses after!) And hurts to smooth over, and deed to applaud …a little girl fell! Where were You, God? A little girl fell! God, why weren't you there?

If you're God at all …then You could have prevented this nightmare of pain! So You must have consented. I've always believed You were loving and good, I'd like to believe still, if only I could.

But God, if You love me, how can You allow such unbearable pain as I'm feeling right now! Such helplessness …helplessness …bitter regret …so many tears that have fallen and yet so many more that are still locked inside.

Oh, God …out there somewhere …have You ever cried? I'm not even sure, anymore that You are real, but if You are God …do You care how I feel?

Beloved, I care! In the midst of your grief, (Daniel 9:23). In the midst of your stricken and crumbling belief (Jeremiah 31:3). In the midst of the blackness of total despair. In the midst of your questioning, Child …*I am there.* (Hebrews 13:5)

"In the midst!" Not far off in some vague fifth dimension, but there, *where you are,* giving you *My* attention. (Psalms 40:17)

My constant attention …and not just today, since before you

were born, I have loved you this way. You're important to *Me*, every hair on your head I have numbered Myself, (Luke 12:7d). Can these tears that you shed (Matthew 10:30) go uncounted? Unnoticed? Nay, Child, here I stand close enough that each teardrop falls into My hand. (Psalms 56:8)

I know what you suffer, I know what you'll gain, if you'll let Me walk with you into your pain. I'll carry your grief, and your sorrow I'll bare. (Isaiah 53) You've only to reach out your hand …I am there.

Fear nothing for your Janet, your dear little girl (John 14:1–3). She is safe in My house, and all Heaven's awhirl with the ring of her laughter, her quick eager smile, and the things she's saving to show "after a while." Yes, I could have prevented …but, Child, you can't see, with My perfect wisdom, trust Janet to Me.

Of course, you will miss her, but while you are weeping, remember, it's only her body that's sleeping. Her "self" is awake, wide awake, as I said, I am God of the living, not God of the dead. (Matthew 22:32). She trusted Me, and My sure Word comes to pass, "Who believes shall not die." That included your lass. (John 11:25).

Let Me walk with you now, through the long heavy days. Let me slowly begin changing heartache to praise. Take hold of My hand, Child, take hold of My love. I will lead you to joys that you yet know not of. Your faith may be weak, and your trust incomplete. (Matthew 12:20). But I'll not walk too fast for your stumbling feet. (Psalms 103:14).

(This was written by the mother who lost her eight-year-old daughter …murdered on her way to school).

God had been gracious in His loving kindness toward all these children of His in their time of heartache, and now they were able to reach out to us and share with us out of their deep well of experience. We enjoyed many drinks of fresh water drawn from these Valley of Baca trials. Psalms 84:5–7(KJV), says, "Blessed is the man whose strength is in Thee: in whose heart are the ways of them: Who passing through the Valley of Baca make it a well: the rain also filleth the pools. They go from strength to strength; every one of them in Zion appeareth before God."

One of the greatest evangelists of our generation, Dr. Vance Havner, came to our home for lunch one day. A friend, Pat Berryhill, and I had prepared a real old fashioned "southern cooking" meal. I made sure that everything was ready before he arrived. As I greeted him at the door, so honored to have such a godly man in our home, I asked him not to say anything unless I was right there at his feet to hear it. I asked him to share something with me that God had shown him that had helped him the most in his spiritual walk. He told us about how he had struggled with the circumstances of his dear wife's long illness and ultimate death. He had asked God to heal her. His faith was strong, as he believed that God knew how dependent he was on her, not only as a supportive helpmate, but also as a traveling partner. She had driven him to all his speaking engagements and revival meetings in their Buick for all their years together. He was simply unable to get into an airplane. With his marvelous dry humor, he told us that God had said, "Lo, I will be with you always." So he dared not go up high in anything. But God, in His wisdom, did not will that she should be healed. Dr. Vance was brokenhearted. He made his way to the Psalms for solace. There he found comfort in the discovery again of the Baca testimony. Baca means sorrow. And so I will paraphrase this as I remember his interpretation.

As you go through the trials and sorrows in your life, dig a well. Dig it deep. Someone else will come down through this same valley and will need a drink. You will be able to share with them that which will refresh their spirits, and point them to the Living Water, Jesus Christ our Lord.

Dr. Havner has since joined his precious wife in Heaven. It will be such joy when we arrive on our appointed day, to see our Savior face to face, and then to join with the giants of the faith, like the Havners, singing praises to the King of Kings and Lord of Lords, the Savior of our souls even Jesus Christ, the Lord. Hallelujah!

For many years, I have received so many blessings and such encouragement from reading *Our Daily Bread* put out by the Radio Bible Class. This past week, the thought for the day was centered around "Calamity or Blessing." The writer told a story about General "Stonewall" Jackson losing his arm in battle. His chaplain exclaimed, "Oh, General, what a calamity!"

Jackson thanked him for his sympathy, but replied, "You see me wounded, but not depressed, not unhappy. I believe it has been according to God's holy will, and I acquiesce entirely in it. You may think it strange, but you never saw me more perfectly contented that than I am today, for I am sure my heavenly Father designs this affliction for my good. I am perfectly satisfied that either in this life or in that which is to come, I shall discover that which is now regarded as calamity is a blessing."

The writer included a verse written by an anonymous believer:

> *As we travel through life's shadowed valley,*
> *Fresh springs of God's love ever rise,*
> *And we learn that our sorrow and losses*
> *Are blessings He sent in disguise. Anon.*

This was precisely what Dr. Havner had discovered. This was what the mother of the murdered child had finally understood. This, indeed, is our testimony. *God is too loving to be mean and too wise to make a mistake.* We are in His care.

> "And we know that all things work together for good to them that love God, to them who are called according to his purpose." Romans 8:28

> "In all these things we are more than conquerors, through Him that loved us. For I am persuaded that neither death, nor life, nor angels, nor principalities, nor powers, nor things present nor things to come, nor height nor depth, nor any other creature, shall be able to separate us from the love of God, which is in Christ Jesus, our Lord." Romans 8:37–39

God has opened many doors already for our family to share with hurting people out of our experience. He has been so faithful to meet every single need of our lives; how could we do less than tell and show others how they can come unto Him and receive for themselves all that He is and all that He has for them.

First things first: You must come to Him by faith, receiving Him as your own personal Lord and Savior. Are you asking, "How is this possible?" Romans 3:23 says, *"For all have sinned and come short of the glory of God."* We must accept God's assessment of our spiritual state. *I am a sinner.*

Romans 6:23a says, *"the wages of sin is death."* This death is a spiritual death, separation forever from God. We earned this by giving over our lives to our selfish desires throughout our years.

Romans 5:8 says, *"But God commended His love toward us, in that, while we were yet sinners, Christ died for us."* God, being the

Holy and perfect God, is unable to be in the presence of sinful man. Yet He loves us and longs for fellowship with us. He *had* to provide the sinless, spotless Lamb of God, His only begotten Son, Jesus Christ, to be the sacrifice for our sins. What amazing grace; we break His heart over and over, and He still loves us and died for us.

Romans 6:23b gives us the good news, *"But the gift of God is eternal life through Jesus Christ our Lord."*

Ephesians 2:8–9 says, *"For by grace you have been saved through faith, and that not of yourselves; it is the gift of God; not of works, lest any man should boast."*

You can do absolutely nothing to merit this grace. It is a gift. If you earned any part of it, it would no longer be a gift. You simply must receive it for yourself. No one can do that for you. Faith is what must be acted upon. And faith is, very simply, believing God. If God says that the blood of His Son was shed to cover all sins of man, past, present and future, then that is exactly what happened that day nearly two thousand years ago on Calvary's Cross. Satan used men to do the vilest work imaginable—crucify God's Love Gift. But God did the most magnanimous thing imaginable when He spoke from the Tree and said, *"Father, forgive them, for they know not what they do."* And then ultimately, He cried, *"It is finished!"* Full atonement had been made for our sin. Three days later, He came forth from the grave, proclaiming to us all the final victory over death and hell.

"I am the resurrection and the life; he that believeth in me, though he were dead, yet shall he live; and whosoever liveth and believeth in me shall never die. Believest thou this?" John 11:25–26 (KJV)

The ball is in our court now. What will you do with God's offer to you? Romans 10:9–10, 13 tells you what to do next if you want to say yes to Jesus.

> "That if you confess with your mouth the Lord Jesus and believe in your heart that God has raised Him from the dead, you will be saved. For with the heart one believes unto righteousness, and with the mouth confession is made unto salvation. For whoever calls on the name of the Lord shall be saved." Romans 10:9–10, 13

> "He came unto His own, and His own received Him not. But as many as received Him, to them gave He power to become the sons of God, even to them that believe on His name." John 1:11–12 KJV

With a sincere heart, confess to God that you are a sinner. Ask Him to forgive your sins. Thank Him for dying for you. Ask Him to help you to live for Him the rest of your days upon this earth. Praise Him for salvation that is for all eternity. Pray in Jesus' name, and on the basis of His shed blood, and believing His Word, claim your new status, a redeemed child of God. Now walk accordingly!

Without the presence of God Himself in your life, I do not know how anyone would be able to get through the crises like the one I've talked about in this book. But with the Lord, we know that even when we pass through the waters, He will be with us. "And *when we pass through the rivers, they will not sweep over us. When we walk through the fire we will not be burned; the flames will not set us ablaze.*" God told us this in Isaiah 43:2–3- sealing it with *"For I am the Lord, your God, the Holy One of Israel, your Savior."* He is able! He is willing! He is God!

"The Lord is the everlasting God, the Creator of the

ends of the earth. He will not grow tired or weary, and His understanding no one can fathom. He gives strength to the weary and increases the power of the weak. Even youths grow tired and weary, and young men stumble and fall; but those who hope in the Lord will renew their strength. They will soar on wings like eagles; they will run and not grow weary, they will walk and not be faint." Isaiah 40:28b-31 NIV

Luke records Jesus reading about Himself from the scrolls in the synagogue. He read from Isaiah 61:1–3- "The Spirit of the Sovereign Lord is on me, because the Lord has anointed Me to preach good news to the poor. He has sent me to bind up the brokenhearted, to proclaim freedom for the captives and release from darkness for the prisoners, to proclaim the year of the Lord's favor. And the day of vengeance of our God, to comfort all who mourn, and provide for those who grieve in Zion - to bestow on them a crown of beauty instead of ashes, the oil of gladness instead of mourning, and a garment of praise instead of a spirit of despair. They will be called oaks of righteousness, a planting of the Lord for the display of His splendor."

My heart cries out, "Amen and amen!" He has done all this and so much more for our family during these special months. It is inconceivable to me that anyone would not rush to Him and receive His gift of salvation if they are lost. It is equally hard to believe how many of His children are living frustrated and defeated lives. They are trying to make it through each day in their own strength, quenching the Holy Spirit within resulting in a grieved personality without. All these promises and all this power is available and they are not claiming them. I pray that this will be a decision time for the reader. Today is the day of salvation.

IO. *The Faithfulness of God and His Sustaining Grace*

As critical as the Word of God is to getting through a sudden crisis; and as soothing as it is to be ministered to by the family of God; perhaps your real stability hinges on how deep your roots go when it comes to believing what God says about our future.

When I saw that God's Word was truth when He said, "Come unto Me, all ye who labor and are heavy laden and I will give you rest," and I did what He said and experienced His rest; I have had little trouble believing the other things I've read in the Bible. This happened at conversion. It has continued to prove itself to be infallible throughout my sanctified walk.

The Bible says so much to us about what God has planned for us after this brief little life span expires.

We are taught that we are a spirit. God breathes life into our spirits. Our spirits are housed in our physical bodies. Each one of us has a soul, which has a mind, emotions, and a will. Every human being has a built in need to know his creator. It has been called a heart-shaped vacuum that can only be filled by

Jesus Christ. All through our lives, we are fed through our minds, much that is good and profitable, and much that is evil and garbage. What is fed into the mind directly affects the emotions, and then the will exercises itself either toward the good or the bad.

If, after hearing about God's love for us and His plan for our life, we respond in faith, receiving His gift of salvation, the Holy Spirit of God Himself comes to live in our hearts. He immediately begins the ministry of leading us into all truth. That truth sets us free from doubt, fear, anxiety, self-pity, depression, bitterness and all of the other negatives that would normally paralyze us.

The truth is that Jesus said in John 14:1–3 - *"Let not your heart be troubled; believe in God, believe also in Me. In My Father's house are many dwelling places; if it were not so, I would have told you; for I go to prepare a place for you. And if I go and prepare a place for you, I will come again, and receive you to Myself; that where I am, there you may be also."*

Jesus showed us a comforting truth when He met Martha, who was very upset that He had not arrived earlier and prevented her brother Lazarus from dying. He said to her, *"Your brother shall rise again. I am the resurrection and the life; he who believes in Me shall live even if he dies, and everyone who lives and believes in Me shall never die. Do you believe this?"*

When the Bible speaks about our having eternal life, we have the assurance that we have God's life in us, and that life has no end. This life is but a short period of time. We know that when it comes to its end, our spirits are still very much alive and according to the scripture, we simply absent ourselves from this body and are immediately present with the Lord. We will live throughout eternity in His presence. In I Thessalonians 4:13–18- we are told not to be uninformed about what happens to those we love who have died. *"For if we believe that Jesus died and rose again, even so God will bring with Him those who have fallen asleep in Jesus. For this we say to you by the word of the Lord, that we who are alive, and remain until the coming of the Lord, shall not precede those who have fallen asleep. For the Lord Himself will descend from heaven with a shout, with the voice of the archangel, and with the trumpet of God; and the dead in Christ shall rise first. Then we who are alive and remain shall be caught up together with them in the clouds to meet the Lord in the air, and thus we shall always be with the Lord. Therefore, comfort one another with these words."*

What a comfort it is to know that there will be this great reunion day. As we see more of the people we love going on to be with the Lord, we better understand what Paul, the apostle, was wrestling with when he said, "For me to live is Christ and to die is gain."

Not only will we finally look into the precious face of our Lord Jesus, but we will also see beyond Him all those loved ones who have gone on before us. We don't know that much about the details of what Heaven will be like, but we do know that we will be like Jesus. We will see things finally as He has seen them all along. We know from the insight we got from the recorded Mount of Transfiguration experience that we will recognize each other in our resurrected bodies. We saw that many recognized Jesus during the days following His resurrection. We know He talked and ate. We know He was not limited as He was when He was in His earthly body.

I believe that everything we have recorded in the gospels about Jesus and His ministry has been put there for us to see how He deals with us now and what He has for us in the future. I remember coming across the account of Jesus' encounter with the funeral procession coming out of Jerusalem. The only son of a widow of Nain had died. His mother's heart was broken. She had known the loneliness without her husband. But her son had given her life meaning and purpose. Losing him was too much for her to bear. The contrast between two groups of people that day teaches us a great lesson. One group was enveloped in darkness and despair. Weeping and wailing were the sounds from their voices. Their faces showed their hopelessness.

The other group had the Son of God in their midst. Where He was there was light and life. The crowd had just witnessed Him healing a centurion's servant. They had seen Him exercise power over disease, demons, and death. There was joy in His presence and hope in their hearts.

Luke tells us that when Jesus saw this grief-stricken widow, He felt compassion for her and said to her, "Do not weep." And He came up and touched the coffin; and the bearers came to a halt. And He said, "Young man, I say to you, arise." And the dead man sat up and began to speak. And Jesus gave him back to his mother.

She thought she would never hear words from his lips again. But Jesus came by that day and brought life and light to bear upon them. I am quite sure hopelessness never again was in their vocabulary.

What I believe this says to us today is that one day when Debbie dies, or if Jesus raptures His church before that, Jesus, who felt compassion for her just as surely as He did for the widow of Nain, will personally give Tiffany back to her mother. And, of course, I mean to Skip and Garrett, too. And the rest of us who love them all so very much will fill Heaven with extra praise to the Lamb Who made this possible.

How wonderful it will be to have my turn come to hold her and hug and kiss her again. It will no longer be a still cold body. The new body will be filled with her spirit again. We won't speak to a lifeless body that is unable to respond. She will laugh again and chatter forth telling all of us her own special personal Jesus story.

In the meantime, I'll return to what Paul said in Philippians: "For me to live is Christ and to die is gain. But if I am to live on in the flesh, this will mean fruitful labor for me." And again he said, "I do not regard myself as having laid hold of it yet; but one thing I do, forgetting what lies behind and reaching forward to what lies ahead, I press on toward the goal of the prize of the upward call of God in Christ Jesus."

So much yet to do; so little time to accomplish it. But we must all be busy about our Father's business until He comes.

Even so, come Lord Jesus!

Yes, I am confident of this very thing, that He who began a good work in us will perfect it until the day of Christ Jesus.

We are comforted by the Word of God within us; by the people of God surrounding us; and by the hope of glory ahead us. And this is the secret of being prepared when the crisis comes suddenly, unexpectedly from out of nowhere. Your life is not built on sand, but on the Rock. The Rock is Jesus. And you stand and you withstand all the circumstances that come your way. And you keep on looking unto Jesus, the author and finisher of your faith.

II. *Conclusion*

At the time that I finished writing *From Silent Tears*, five years had passed since the accident. It had taken me almost two and one half years to get this much of my book written. I thought it would be a simple process.

Just pour my heart out, get someone to type it and someone to edit it, find a publisher and get on with sharing comfort with others going through their personal crisis. It was not that easy. I came to many blocks along the way.

The toughest place of all has been this conclusion. I seemed to be finding a million excuses to keep me from finishing something that I had started with such fervor. It made no sense to me that I was making this into a major mountain that I could not climb.

One day I heard about a family whose daughter was traveling from Florida to Huntsville to surprise them. They got that unexpected call telling them that she had been in a car accident and was killed.

My heart breaks every time I hear of someone going through this terrifying time. My friend, Brenda McDaniel, was working with the family about funeral arrangements. She called and asked me if I would go to their home and minister to them. They were new in Huntsville and didn't have a church family or close friends. Of course I went to them to let them know that I knew something about how they were hurting. I told them that I knew they were new in Huntsville. I wanted them to know that there were people all around who cared about them and wanted desperately to minister to them in some way. I told them about God saying that after we have experienced a trial, we are to share the comfort He leaves with us with others going through similar trials.

In the middle of our little visit, I said that I wished that I had my little book finished so that I could give them a copy, but that I had not been able to get the last bit of it written. I needed the right conclusion. The husband stepped into the room and said, "You have the conclusion. Tell them about that Baca thing." (Psalm 84:6) So that is what I'm doing.

Whatever you might be going through in your life right now, I recommend that rather than sitting in a pool of self-pity or ranting and raving at everyone around, including God, start digging your well. God will cross your path many times with others going through like trials. You don't have to have tons of scripture memorized, although that is so helpful to you. You simply have to share your testimony as to how God worked in your life and brought you through to the victory side. Nothing will give you more joy, except being able to lead someone to Jesus Christ in a salvation experience.

Another thing that is very important to me to get across here is that everyone will not go through their trial exactly the same way.

You often hear about the five stages of grief a person *must* go through in order to come out on the other side emotionally sound. Elizabeth Kubler-Ross, who is considered to be an authority on the stages of death and dying, describes the grief process like this:

1. Bargaining ...Plead with God before death to let someone live.

2. Denial ...Avoiding reality ...allowing yourself time to collect yourself.

3. Anger ...rage, envy, resentment, and uncontrolled emotion.

4. Depression ...Drained emotions, hopelessness, and despair.

5. Acceptance ...Void of feeling ...able to recover and enter into normal roles again.

In my experience, this has not been so. Tiffany, my parents, my brother and sister, my brother-in-law, and some very close friends have died. It has never crossed my mind that I should be angry with God or hate my departed loved one for a moment. I have not been "depressed," nor have I denied that they were, indeed, dead. I have missed them terribly. I have picked up the phone to call them, because this had been such a lovely weekly touch. I have cried when a memory came that was intensely painful. But as my daughter said wisely, "You cry when you need to, but then you suck it up and get on with living."

My family joins me in saying that this has been their experience, also. I don't think we are all naive or that we are carrying excess baggage around that is going to rise up and haunt us one day.

I simply think that this comes from believing God; accepting His Sovereignty; knowing that He is too loving to be mean and too wise to make a mistake.

We have gone to the throne room in our time of need and received from Him the Grace Package designed especially for us. It never came up short. He was always faithful to meet our deep needs and to satisfy our souls in the process. His desire is to do the same for all His children.

Weeping was for the night, but joy did come in the "mourning."

It is just as important for me to communicate to you that if you do need to go through a grief cycle, and come out on the other side praising God and committing yourself anew to serving Him with all your strength and loving Him with all your soul, you will hear a "Well done, good and faithful servant," also.

So, it is not so much exactly how we got through, but that we got through and that we dug a good and deep well. Blessings will flow from our own experiences and touch the lives of multiplied thousands around us.

Jesus will be lifted up!

Glory will go to our Father's Name!

We will say with Job, *"But he knoweth the way that I take; when He hath tested me, I shall come forth as gold."* (Job 23:10) Those who bless God in their trials will be blessed by God through their trials. I can say sincerely, *Amen.*

This event happened several years after *From Silent Tears* was completed. I got a call from Bro. Herman Pair one day. You will remember him as the pastor of the church Debbie and Skip attended. He told me that there had been a tragic accident, and he knew that we would be interested in knowing about it. Jo Taylor's granddaughter had fallen off her bicycle and hit her head. The little girl died, and her family was devastated. My heart broke as memories flooded my mind. Jo had told us that when she saw Tiffany's lifeless body, she could see her little three-year-old blonde headed granddaughter. She vowed then that she would never take another day for granted. She would spend precious time with her even if it meant cutting back on her responsibilities at her job. She told me later that she had not missed any of the special occasions since.

It took me quite a while, but I finally found a telephone number for Jo. She had changed to another nursing home. They gave me her son's home number. The first time I called, Jo was not there. I had a long talk with her son. I was able to talk to Jo the next time I called. Of course, the whole family was in such pain. I asked Jo if she remembered what she said to us after Tiffany's death. She said that she remembered every detail. I asked her if she had thought about how gracious it was of God to put her in that place so that she could see how very important it is for us to see each day as a gift from God to be used rightly by keeping our priorities in order. He had shown Jo how to value each day she had with her little granddaughter. So many people face tragedies like this having to admit that if they could do things over again, they would not waste a minute of the valuable time they have with their loved ones.

Tiffany with Raggedy Ann And Raggedy Andy,
a Christmas gift made by
Aunt Jane, 1987.

Skip, Debbie, Garrett, and Tiffany, 1987

Garrett, 1996

Debbie, 1994

Tiffany snuggled on Poppy's shoulder

Laddie and Rita, Garrett, and Tiffany
35th Wedding Anniversary
September 21, 1987

Debbie, Garrett, and Laddie
Debbie's Birthday, 1995

Grandmother Ree
With her little joys,
1987

Garrett (4 ½), Tiffany (2), And Ree
(This was the last little dress I made for Tiff)

Book II

Hammered Gold

I. *Faith Through Feast and Famine*

Perry and Marilyn Calvert

As I reflect back on the genesis of this project, I remember how sure I was that I needed to put together a sampling of testimonies of some of the people I knew who had gone through various kinds of severe trials and yet their witness through their experience was powerfully positive. This would be the encouragement I felt was needed for those who read *From Silent Tears* and thought that they could not have gotten through what we experienced with Tiffany's death. The Calverts came to my mind as friends who had been extraordinary witnesses to God's faithfulness in the area of finances.

Little did I know that when I finally sat down with them for their interview, I would find myself totally surprised and shocked to discover just how deep their faith indeed was. I had absolutely no clue that they had been in the process, (having gone through the purifying of the gold in the fire), of now learning about the hammering of the gold. But it is in the hammering that the gold becomes transparent and you see Jesus Christ shining through them. Marilyn told me right up front that when I heard what they had to share, I might not want to put it in this book. I assured her that I believed God laid them on my heart, and that was confirmed by their willingness to be a part of this. After they poured out their story, I assured them that this was indeed exactly the kind of testimony I needed. For you to read on is for you to be richly blessed!

We'll go back to 1975 and the first Capital Stewardship Program being launched at Whitesburg Baptist Church. Phase I was to buy the Mormon Church, parking lots, and the architectural drawings. Perry was asked to lead the church in this endeavor. Prior to the kick off, Perry attended a Manley Beasley Retreat, the focus of which was *Walking by Faith*. There was a session on faith and giving which was to be life changing for him. He recalled the text and the key points: The Church at Macedonia (II Corinthians 9):

1. The Macedonians first gave themselves to the Lord.
2. Then they gave out of their own resources.
3. Then they gave out of God's resources.

The thought kept burning in his mind and spirit, "What could God do if one man yielded completely in this area, signing his name to a blank contract; any place, anything God wanted to do with him, *He could do?*"

The time came to lead out in the Stewardship emphasis

with Perry and Marilyn's pledge. As was their practice, Perry listened for God to let him know the amount through his morning prayer and Bible study time. He spends the first one to two hours in the morning seeking God. Decisions were never made based on emotions, but were made based on faith in what God put light on in His Word. God gave him a clear vision of what he was to do. Even though Perry had a very lucrative income, he knew immediately that God would have to be the One Who made this happen. For the next three years, God worked supernaturally through them to meet the commitment they had made to this building fund. And it was done week by week. It was not unusual for them to write the check to put in the offering without having the funds to cover it. They would go to the post office box, and there would be the amount needed at that eleventh hour. Each week they had the faith challenge of believing what the checkbook said or what God said. No problem there, God would always win out. At the end of the campaign, five times the amount they had pledged had been given, and all the praise and credit went to Him. For the next year they chose to just continue to give the weekly gift to the future building fund as God provided. [Wow, now what do you think about that? This bracketed text is something I, Rita, want to share with you. A few years ago, I was privileged to sit at the feet of Dr. John Phillips, an anointed writer of commentaries. He shared with us that when you are reading the Psalms and come to the word Selah, he translates it to mean, "Wow, what do you think about that? There are several times I've felt like that response was appropriate while writing this chapter.

Now a new campaign started. Phase II was the building of the new Worship Center. Once again, Perry entered into his prayer closet to discern what God would have them pledge this time. Surely He would expect them to do no less than they had done before. It would make spiritual sense to do even more. Perry took a legal pad and began listing an inventory of all their assets. There was their lovely home, bank stock, real estate, cash value on his life insurance and their retirement fund. After totaling it, he asked Marilyn if she would be willing to sell everything they owned and give to the church in order to be obedient to God. Her answer was, "Yes, if you feel it's what God wants." Marilyn added something here that was so special. She said that she knew Perry's walk with God was so close that she could give that answer with peace in her heart. The next morning in his prayer time, he said, "Lord, you know I have to have an answer today." The scripture he read that morning said, "Go, do all that is in your heart, for the Lord is with you." Filled with renewed faith and confidence in their God Who never fails to keep His word, they launched out again in their biggest step of faith yet. (Wow, what do you think about that!)

God gave Perry another promise in Mark 10:29–30 (KJV):

"Verily I say unto you, there is no man that hath left house or brethren, or sisters, or father, or mother, or wife, or children, or lands, for my sake, and the gospel's, but he shall receive a hundredfold now in this time, houses, and brethren, and sisters and mothers, and children, and lands, with persecutions; and in the world to come eternal life."

Another important promise Perry received from God through the scriptures was found in Isaiah 50:7 (KJV):

"For the Lord God helps me, therefore I am not disgraced. Therefore, I have set my face like flint, and I know that I shall not be ashamed."

The Calverts have two very special children; Mike, who is a minister of the Gospel, and Dana, a devoted wife and mother. When asked about how they felt about their parents committing to possibly giving up all their material possessions, their quick response was that their parents could not give away their real inheritance, which is theirs in Jesus Christ. That kind of maturity speaks so loudly as to the witness of these two parents to their children through the years. Like their mother, they had the utmost confidence in the father's ability to discern God's will in their lives.

Within four weeks of the kick-off of this Phase II Stewardship emphasis, the testing time began. A lawsuit was filed against Perry concerning a piece of real estate he had bought from a man who did not have the right to sell it. Ultimately Perry was exonerated and declared to still be the owner of the property, but it had taken almost three years to get this settled, and legal fees had mounted.

Perry's business was primarily insurance and mortgage loans. High interest rates destroyed his business. A very large yearly income plummeted. *God got very silent.* As they continued to listen for God to speak to them through their Bible study, the only word they seemed to get was, *"Just wait on me."* For the next three years, every new business venture Perry tried ended up in failure. Their income was one tenth of what it had been.

At this point in the interview, I jumped in and asked them to share with me how they were feeling down in the pits of their stomachs, in the midst of this fire. *Peace* was their quick response. But at the same time, they said that they did spend much time on their knees praying and often crying, and yes, even wondering if they had heard God right. But it never took them long

to remember the promises they had been given. Perry lifted up
Joshua 21:45 (KJV) where it says, *"Not one of the good promises
which the Lord had made to the house of Israel failed; all came to
pass."* And so they continued to trust Him!

At the end of the three year commitment period, having
experienced financial famine, Perry spoke to God, "Lord, we
knew if we were going to make this commitment, you would
have to do it. It looks like we'll need to give everything we own to
the church now." He was driving later that morning and turned
on the radio, and the first thing he heard was this song:

> *I'd rather have Jesus than silver or gold,*
> *I'd rather have Him than have riches untold,*
> *I'd rather have Jesus than houses or lands,*
> *I'd rather be led by His nail pierced hands.*

Peace settled over him like a warm blanket. He couldn't wait
to share this with Marilyn. She agreed that this was from God.
The next morning, driving once again, he turned the radio on
and heard the words, "all the vain things that charm me most, I
sacrifice them to His blood."

On March 28, 1983, Perry and Marilyn moved into an apartment with the same grace and dignity and peace that they had
when they lived in the big house. There was one really funny thing
Marilyn told me about. Before they moved, it was necessary to
deal with having to condense their household things to that which
would fit into a smaller apartment. They had a ton of camping
equipment, tents and things. These were filled with memories of
the times the family had spent in the great outdoors. Marilyn had
commented that they could always live in the tent. While reading
her Bible, she came across a verse that said, *"For Thou hast been a
refuge for me, a tower of strength against the enemy. Let me dwell in*

thy tent forever. Let me take refuge in the shelter of Thy wings" (Psalm 61:3–4 KJV). She laughed when she said she cried out, "Oh, no, Lord, I didn't mean it!" So when the first person came and said they would really like to have the tent and supplies, she hurriedly told them they could gladly have everything free.

Since 1983, several times it would look to them like things were turning around for Perry's business. Then it would be like he hit an invisible wall. With all his will to work and to succeed, no matter how he persevered, things would close down. For nineteen years, there has been no reserve or resources on which to fall back. In fact, three of these years they were unable to afford medical insurance. But God was still faithful! They were in excellent health during that period. God later blessed Marilyn with a job that had the benefit package that they needed.

In May 1997, Perry was tested in a new way. Having enjoyed great health all his life, he found himself in severe neck pain, requiring surgery. For eleven weeks, he was unable to get out to continue to find business. But God knew exactly where he was and did not leave him wanting. During that period, people began to come to their apartment with business. In fact, they said that God blessed them more financially during that period of time than in the nineteen years before.

Perry was scheduled to have the neck surgery, when he got a call from a church in Decatur asking him to do a Capital Stewardship Campaign for them. He delayed the surgery in order to make this money. In excruciating pain, with a neck brace, Marilyn packed him into a van and drove him to Decatur. Perry made her park some distance from the church so that no one would see him looking like an invalid trying to get out of the van. While he was speaking, he reached up and took the brace off so that he could communicate better. God was listening to Marilyn in another room as she was praying for Perry. She prayed Psalm 3:3 over and over, *"He's the lifter of my head."* God not only held Perry's head high, but also used him in a powerful way to bless this church. Marilyn then packed him back into the van, and he suffered severe pain as they traveled back home. They knew God was still keeping His promise that Perry would not be ashamed.

During all of this time, they knew that it would never be a matter of looking to man to meet their needs. They would only look to God to do that. So they did not make their circumstances known to others. This was why it was such a shock to me to hear this story. I have known them for thirty-one plus years. I saw no change in their countenance or their walk with God as they went from affluence to financial crisis. There was no sinking into a pool of self-pity or depression. There was no deviation from their commitment to serve the Lord through the church. If you asked them how things were going when you knew that their extended families were going through health crises, they always had something positive to report. How can you walk so tall and straight for such a long period of time? Where does this kind of strength come from? Oh, listen to me carefully. It has everything to do first of all with the depth of your love and devotion to Jesus Christ. Then it has to do with your having experienced God day by day in that private time you spend with him early in the morning. Add to this your diligence in Bible study, knowing the word of God and doing it. That's the secret!

Listen to a few passages of scripture they shared with me that have meant so much to them. Marilyn's favorite is Psalm 16:11 (KJV):

"Thou wilt make known to me the path of life; in Thy

presence is fullness of joy; on Thy right hand there are pleasures forever."

"For I know the plans that I have for you, declares the Lord, plans for welfare and not for calamity to give you a future and a hope. Then you will call upon Me and come and pray to Me, and I will listen to you. And you will seek Me and find Me, when you search for Me with all your heart." Jeremiah 29:11–13 (NAS)

"Do not fear, for I am with you, for I am your God. I will strengthen you, surely I will help you, surely I will uphold you with My righteous right hand." Isaiah 41:10 (KJV)

"This is the way, walk ye in it." Isaiah 30:21 (KJV) God spoke this through His Word to Marilyn's heart.

They summed it up something like this. *God has been faithful. When material things were scarce, His grace was abundant. We would not trade what God has taught us for all of the money in the world.*

I believe them. I have been so encouraged by them to go deeper than I have been in the area of faith. I was touched by the joy they have each morning when they get up and say to each other; "Today might be the day." What day you might ask? The day when God breaks through and shows them the fulfillment of His promise that there is no man that hath left house or brethren, or sisters, or father, or mother, or wife, or children, or lands, for My sake, and the gospel's, but he shall receive a hundredfold now *in this time,* houses and brethren, and sisters, and mothers, and children, and lands, with persecutions, and in the world to come eternal.

2. *Bridges Over Troubled Waters*

Floyce and Ellen Bridges

One of the best parts about writing this book is the joy of being able to spend a few hours with some of the most special people I know. Ellen and Floyce Bridges are two of these. They have such courageous testimonies of how you can walk through your life trusting in God's faithfulness in spite of your circumstances.

I felt that the best place for me to begin was digging around their family roots. Both of them were raised in Christian homes and were blessed with godly parents. They were raised on farms in Cullman County in Alabama. Born in the depression in the early 1920s, they learned early in their lives how to survive on little in the material realm. As hard as the times were, they had the most important things - love, faith and a secure foundation.

When World War II broke out, Floyce was drafted. Ellen was in the tenth grade in high school. She impressed everyone with her academic excellence. There was one thing that was so important to Floyce. He loved Ellen with all his heart, and she loved him as deeply. He wanted to marry Ellen before he left. He did not know where he would be going or if he would ever return. But he had to know that Ellen would be taken care of if anything should happen to him. In 1940, they secretly married, much to the disappointment of Ellen's family. They loved Floyce, but they wanted Ellen to finish high school and go on to college and get the degree that she deserved.

Much to Ellen's surprise, when she returned to her high school, her principal told her that she could no longer attend classes. This saddened him because he knew her potential was outstanding. However, he felt that this would set a bad example for other students who might decide they would like to get married, also.

Ellen was devastated! Being the strong survivor that she was, she dug her heels in, went to work to make even the smallest wages, gave her husband much needed love and support even from across the ocean, and God took care of them both.

God had a surprise in store for Ellen. There was a lady in Cullman who had a kindergarten. She desperately needed a helper and asked Ellen if she would consider taking the job. She had been told that Ellen was an excellent Sunday school teacher. Ellen felt very inadequate at the time but later realized that God had provided an opportunity for her to learn at the feet of a master kindergarten leader.

Several years later, the Bridges were divinely led to Huntsville, Alabama. This little farming town had been selected by Wernher Von Braun to be the site for the Space Program. Peace and tranquility gave way to booming growth, revealing great needs immediately. Ellen thought about starting a kindergarten in her home. God had other plans for her. The Bridges were charter members of Whitesburg Baptist Church. It was obvious to several families that there was a real need for a church in southeast Huntsville. Some property was bought, and plans were underway to build in a cotton field. While the little church was being built, these families met in the National Guard Armory building. Ellen volunteered to keep the children at her house.

Ellen asked the pastor about the possibility of starting a kindergarten at the church when it was completed. He encouraged her to do some research to see how she would go about this. In January 1959, Ellen saw God's plan fully revealed. Seventeen children enrolled with two teachers, Ellen and Clara Gunter. The enrollment doubled the next year. They have consistently enrolled well over two hundred children each year, and there is always a waiting list. Ellen also started a Mother's Morning Out program. Ellen retired in January, 1994 after thirty-five years of outstanding service.

She shared with me a touching story about not having gotten that degree her family coveted for her. She said that she was like the black sheep of her family because all her siblings got their degrees, and all four of her children got their degrees. Her brother had hard feelings toward her for years because of his disappointment in her choices. She has always contended that she was so busy raising her four children and being a wife that she didn't have time to pursue her education. I loved it when she said that she did not regret her choices a bit because she was still married to the same wonderful man after fifty-six years, and she wouldn't trade that for all the degrees in the world.

Now this does not mean that Ellen Bridges did not continue to take advantage of every opportunity to increase her knowledge of childhood education. She attended every workshop available to her. She taught in conferences in many states. And the most special thing happened just before her brother died. This college professor took Ellen in his arms and said, "Ellen, I'm so proud of you for everything you've accomplished."

All of us who know and love Ellen joined him in expressing how proud we are of everything God has done through her.

Now you might wonder when I'm going to say something about Floyce. He wasn't the kindergarten director, but to many children he might have been a notch above that. This poem written by Arnold Puckett tells the story. Floyce was always waiting outside the kindergarten door to greet the children. If it was raining, he held an umbrella over them to keep them dry. Sunshine or rain, he always had that gentle manner and that sweet smile. Here is the poem:

> *School's Out*
> *Here in Huntsville, Alabama,*
> *At the Whitesburg Baptist Church,*
> *Is a Preschool Child's Department*
> *That no one can besmirch.*
> *Mr. Bridges greets the children*
> *When they arrive each day,*
> *And escorts them right to the door*
> *Which is not far away.*
> *For some reason he was absent*
> *When a little child arrived,*

And saw he was not standing
At his place beside the drive.
The mother had not stopped the car
When she heard her son say,
"We might as well keep going,
There will be no school today."
She hugged her little boy close,
"Why did you say that, Dear?"
He pointed to the curb and said,
"Because God isn't here."

Floyce and Ellen looked forward to their retirement years. Certainly they deserved rest from their years of giving sacrificially of their time, talents and energy. One month after retirement, Ellen went to her doctor to get a routine check up. She was not feeling sick. It was just time to check in and get the go ahead for all the traveling they were planning to do.

Two of their daughters, Diane and Phyllis, live in Huntsville. But their daughter, Melody, and her family are missionaries in Dominica. Jim, their only son, is a minister in rural Washington State. So the Bridges were anxious to do some visiting.

Much to Ellen's surprise, she was told that her blood count was very low. They found blood in her rectum. And the next thing she knew, she was seeing a cancer specialist. This was followed by a visit to the hospital for surgery to remove a cancerous tumor from her colon.

When the doctor told her she had cancer, her response was unusual to say the least. She told him about the article in the *Huntsville Times,* (September 28, 1994), which was just the day before going to the doctor, where the *Times* writer had commended her on her outstanding kindergarten ministry. She said,

"Well, I guess God just wants to clip my wings." This is vintage Ellen. No hysteria. Just faith and confidence in God in the good times and the bad times.

The surgery was performed the next morning. Her room was filled with family and friends. Ellen had a peace that was such an encouragement to all who saw her. A year of chemotherapy followed. Even through this, she missed only one Sunday attending her beloved church. After the year, the colonoscopy showed no sign of cancer.

About the middle of this year of chemo, Floyce woke up one morning with numbness in his right hand. He chose not to pay any attention to the symptoms and went out and picked corn and shucked forty ears. This is vintage Floyce. After some insisting from Ellen, he went to the doctor. Tests were done, revealing the beginning of a stroke. He got there in time to get the blood thinner started that headed off further damage. A catherization was done, and they found 99% blockage of the carotid artery. Surgery on that was successful. The doctor told them that they got to that just before it went into a massive stroke.

David and Melody were home on furlough from Dominica for six months during this time. The garden was ready for harvest, and David was a lifesaver helping to gather the crops. Floyce had to wait several days for the blood to thicken before they could do his surgery. He told David to bring the butter beans to the hospital and he would shell them. After all, he had nothing else to do. Ellen took them home and prepared them for the freezer that night. Both of them felt much better! That's vintage Floyce and Ellen Bridges!

There is a funny story I've told over and over about Ellen. Many years ago we were all at a Deacon's dinner. The husbands usually got their wives a corsage for the affair. Ellen was commenting on mine. Then she said, "I told Floyce, 'Don't get me a corsage. Just get me three tomato plants.'" Practical Ellen saw beyond the night to the tomatoes she would enjoy on a sandwich in a few months. That's vintage Ellen!

After Ellen and Floyce had come through the fire that year following their retirement, I passed them in the sanctuary at church. Ellen stopped me and said something to me that may have been one of the most touching moments I've experienced. She said, "I checked your little book, *From Silent Tears, the Hallelujah Song* out of the Church Library. That book helped me more than any other book I've read to understand and to help others understand how to accept death and to understand it better." She thanked me so warmly for writing it and for the way she said I wove the church and our experience of Tiffany's death through the book. I was so blessed to think that God had permitted me the joy of speaking a little peace to these special friends in their time of need.

I asked Ellen to share with all of us the scripture verse that had helped her most to get through the fiery trials in her life, especially in the last few years. Without hesitating, she said, *"I can do all things through Christ who strengthens me.* Philippians 4:13

Well done, good and faithful servants!

3. *Standing Tall Through It All*

Dr. Herman Sollie

"For I am now ready to be offered, and the time of my departure is at hand. I have fought a good fight, I have finished the race, I have kept the faith. Now there is in store for me the crown of righteousness, which the Lord, the righteous judge, will award to me on that day- and not only to me, but also to all who have longed for His appearing." II Timothy 4:6–8 NIV

This is the testimony of Paul, the Apostle. And it was also the testimony of Herman Sollie at the very end of his earthly life. What a tremendous man of faith he was! He inspired many of us to aim for higher ground in our personal walk with Jesus Christ. I pray that all of us who knew him will be found as faithful when we come to our time of departure from this life to our perfected life in Heaven.

Dr. Sollie's daughter, Jo Karr, has been a friend for many years. It was through her that I first heard of her father. There was a horrible trial that came suddenly into their family's life in 1966. Someone came into Jo's sister's home in Tallahassee, Florida, and brutally murdered three members of this family of five. The bodies of Helen, her husband, Dr. R. W. Sims, and their youngest daughter, Joy, were discovered by their two other daughters, Jenny and Judy. They had been stabbed, strangled and shot to death. Even though Helen was brain dead, she was put into the Intensive Care Unit for several days. The hope was that the murderer would think she might survive and be able to identify him.

What amazed me about these days was that Dr. Sollie did not spend them sitting over in a corner saying, "Why me, God? I've been your servant for many years. Why let this happen to my loved ones?" It was just the opposite. His heart went out to the other families in the ICU who were hurting for someone special to them. So he just automatically reached out with a compassionate heart, sharing with them that comfort the Holy Spirit had given him.

His family had trusted Jesus Christ through many hard times. Jenny and Judy had also been raised to know Jesus personally and to trust Him to give to them His sustaining grace. And He did not fail to be true to His word. They knew that if anything should happen to their parents, they were to go to live with Jo and Jim Karr. They did just that and found nurturing comfort with this extended family. Jenny and Judy's testimonies are so strong today. They say, "At our early age, we knew something very few Christians know for sure.... *God is sufficient!*"

Even though the murders were never solved, this family kept on keeping on. Both daughters married Christian husbands and have been blessed with beautiful children. All of them serve the Lord through church ministries.

Now let me back up to a much earlier time in Herman Sollie's life. His father was Methodist, and his mother was Presbyterian. He laughingly said that when the sons learned to read the Bible, they became Baptists. He went so far as to answer God's call to preach the Gospel of Jesus Christ at the age of sixteen. He pastored his first little church when he was eighteen years old and married his sweetheart, Maureen, when he was nineteen.

Dr. Sollie was blessed with a brilliant mind. He attended Howard College, (now known as Samford University), in Birmingham, Alabama. After leaving Howard, he went to Southern Mississippi, where he graduated. Off he and Maureen went to seminary in New Orleans, and back to Southern Mississippi to earn his Master's degree. With a passion for study, he then went to the University of Alabama and earned his doctorate there. He excelled academically and enjoyed teaching English and psychology. While he was at Southern Mississippi teaching some classes, he was also pastoring a small church. He did not feel right about being paid by the church since he was actually teaching on some of their time. So even though he had a family who needed the money, he gave his salary to the church. Integrity was just one of the noble characteristics of this special man.

I know I'm hop, skip and jumping from place to place. However, I'm not interested in the chronology of these years. I'm interested in the testimonials of this man. One such comes to my mind now. While they were in Birmingham attending Howard College, a couple of incidents stand out as exhibits of real faith.

Jo said that times were so difficult for them financially that it kept them on their knees quite a bit. At one point the money ran out totally. Herman confided in a friend that he had no option but to leave Howard.

The friend said, "Why did you come here to begin with?"

Herman replied, "To prepare myself to preach."

The friend asked, "Who called you?"

Herman quickly answered, "God!"

"Then," said the friend, "you must have called yourself if you can un-call yourself, but if God called you, He'll provide!"

There were two particular needs they were praying for: food and a coat for Maureen. With a new perspective as a result of the challenging truth his friend confronted him with, Herman called his little family to get on their knees and pray and give thanks for what God was going to do. There was a knock on their door. He opened the door, and someone from the A&P grocery store offered him a job for the afternoons and evenings, just what he needed to be able to earn food money and continue with his classes during the day. A short time later, there was another knock on their door. This time a man was standing there with a coat. He had gotten his wife a new coat and wondered if they might be able to use this one. God had indeed heard their prayers and provided their needs. Again they went to their knees to give thanks to their Father.

Another story was told to me about Dr. Sollie and his friend, Bro. James Bryan. Now this name will be familiar to all residents of Birmingham, Alabama, and many of us beyond there. I have always heard that this one man touched more lives, especially the down-and-outs, than any other single person in that city. I have heard that it was not unusual at all to see him sitting on a park bench or walking in the coldest kind of weather without a coat, hat or even shoes. He was not eccentric. He just gave these articles of clothing away to someone he met who needed them. Of course, his church always made sure that they replaced these things for him. He just loved the Lord so much that this love then overflowed to those less fortunate than most. You would most likely find him talking to the down-and-outs. When he died, the city mourned from the society to the slums. A statue of Bro. Bryan was placed in Magnolia Park in Birmingham as a reminder to all its citizens of how one man can make such a difference when he walks solely by faith in the one true living God. Everyone who knew him revered him.

I got a little sidetracked from my story, but this testimony fits the purpose of this book perfectly. Dr. Sollie asked him to go with him one night to preach to his little church out from Birmingham. As they got on their way, they realized the need for gas. As the attendant pumped the gas, Sollie apologized to Bro. Bryan when he realized that he did not have enough money to pay for it. Bro. Bryan said that he did not have any money either, but not to worry, the Lord would provide. A man walked up and spoke to Bro. Bryan, "I've been looking for you to give you something. Would it be all-right if I pay for your gas?" This was no surprise to Bro. Bryan. You see, he lived daily by faith, and had always found God to be faithful to His Word. He promised that He had already provided for all our needs pertaining to life and godliness.

Now let's skip over many years later to when Maureen's health began to decline. It was then that Dr. Sollie thought it would be prudent to move to Alabama to retire near Jo and her family. However, retirement never slowed him down. He had been encouraged to make this move by an old friend, J. Otis King, who was well known to preach sermons guaranteed to make you think twice about the necessity of getting right with God *today!* J. Otis told Herman there was a need for good preachers in this area. Sollie, in his seventies by this time, loved the sound of that because he was always ready to stand in a pulpit day or night.

This physically strong giant of a man eventually began to experience his worst nightmare. His health began to decline. Ultimately he was diagnosed with a cancer that caused him to be in excruciating pain. In the last months, there was also the inevitable memory loss. This really frustrated him. However, when given the opportunity to stand behind a pulpit, he amazed everyone. The obvious power and anointing of God was so evident in his preaching that he enjoyed total recall of his message.

In the last month of his life here, Jo said he would be sitting in his chair in a quiet mode. Then he would begin to share what he was seeing with his spirit eyes. It was so beautiful …green, green pastures and crystal clear water. He saw all these absolutely contented people all around. Jo asked him if he recognized anyone. His answer was that he didn't recognize a single one of them. Now this makes all of us who knew him laugh because he had such a wonderful sense of humor.

Another funny story was when he was in the hospital toward the end. His brother, Vernon, was there with some other family members. Dr. Sollie asked Vernon, "If you were going to die, how would you want to go?"

Vernon answered, "A heart attack. How about you?"

Dr. Sollie said, "Slow, drawn out, people all around weeping, and then I'm not going to go!"

When Sollie died, Vernon recalled this and said, "Well, he did it!"

This story Jo told me was hysterical. Bro. Jimmy Jackson, his pastor at Whitesburg Baptist Church, went to the hospital to visit Dr. Sollie.

Sollie said, "Pastor, I want to give a gift for whatever need you have."

Bro. Jimmy suggested the Family Fellowship Fund to help church members going through tough times might be a real need.

Sollie told Jo to write a check for $1000.00, and to repeat that each month. Bro. Jimmy called Jo outside the room and asked if he should not cash the check. Jo said that was what her daddy wanted to do, so go ahead and cash it, but don't expect it each month. Well, that's the way he was; at the very end, thinking of the needs of others more than his own needs.

Those of us who were blessed to know him loved him and miss his presence with us. But his spirit of faith and of selflessness, of genuine compassion, and of serving the Lord with gladness will always remain as a testimony to the way we all should live out our lives here on this earth. In Jesus Christ, he lived and moved and had his being. Amen!

I thought I had finished this chapter when Jo shared a letter with me that I feel should be included. This is a book dealing with the awesome testimonies of many godly men and women. All of these have gone through intense fiery trials. A common thread in each story is their victory in the midst of the fire because of their confidence in the sustaining grace of our Lord Jesus Christ. I draw your attention back to the horror of that night in Tallahassee, Florida, when three members of the Sims family were brutally murdered. Most surviving loved ones would struggle maybe for the rest of their lives with bitterness and anger over these crimes being unsolved. The two daughters kept their eyes on God and claimed the power that was theirs because the Holy Spirit of God abided in them. They not only survived intact, but their testimonies continue to be a blessing to everyone who knows them. Read this letter Judy wrote to the community they had lived in.

May 30, 1997

I am Judy Sims. Over the past 30 years I have thought of the loss of my parents and younger sister practically every day, to some degree. The circumstances surrounding their deaths have changed me forever, but have not destroyed me.

A terrible event that remains a mystery is not the focus of my thoughts most of the time. I think about whom R.W., Helen and Joy, the individuals, would have been at different times in their lives. As I have passed the ages of my parents when they died, I have realized how very young they were. As I realize how old Joy would be today, 43, I think about how close we would have been. In other words, I miss their presence in my life.

God has been so good to me though. He brought me through the shock and grief surrounding their murders with the help of other family members, especially my aunt and uncle, Jo and Jim Karr. They became the grandparents for my children. The loss of my family members has given me great empathy for others who have lost family members in whatever circumstances.

Music has remained an important part of my life. I have

taught piano for the past 25 years, and I am a church organist.

I have a very happy life with a wonderful husband and children. My sister, Jenny, and I are very close.

I don't consider it my goal in life to figure out who murdered my family or to seek revenge. My goal is to live a life that would honor their memory and provide as good a heritage for my children as my parents, R.W. and Helen Sims, provided for me. (Written by Judy Prestage)

Once again, I will have to write a postscript. Jo Karr joined her father and mother, sister, brother-in-law and niece, and many dear friends in Heaven in April of 1998. What a reunion that must have been. The greatest joy of all was when Jo saw Jesus face to face. She loved Him and served Him all the days of her life. Such a crowd of people came to her memorial service. They had all been touched in some special way by her warm way of reaching out to Christians and non-Christians alike. Like her father, the commitment she made as a child was real until she finished the course. It was not always easy. She had multiple health problems. Diabetes had caused her to lose a large part of a foot. Even her husband said that she very seldom ever complained, even when the pain must have been so severe. She loved the ministry she had at Whitesburg Baptist Church. She was in charge of public relations. Working with the youth was one of her real joys. She played a major part in the success of the *I Love America* productions each Fourth of July. She directed weddings for many years. And there was so much more! We will miss her greatly! But we will see her soon.

4. *Faith and Focus*

Hilda Waddell

Through my very good friend, Ramsey Plott Williams, it was my good fortune to meet her mother, Hilda Waddell. The times that I was privileged to visit with her, I immediately discerned that this was indeed one of the godliest women I had ever met. As I learned more about her life, I realized that she proved a truth that I had been teaching for years. This truth is that God has always consistently used three tools to grow His children deep in their faith. The tools are prayer, Bible study and suffering.

The reason that most Christians fail to stand firm when circumstances that severely test their faith come against them is that they do not have time to spend alone with God in prayer. They need the extra sleep in the morning. They are too busy during the day. And they are just too tired and can't stay awake at night. So they ignore the fact that God makes His presence known to us when we draw near to Him. All of us need to know God better, and the way that happens is when we spend time with Him. Praising God and worshipping Him in this private closet time fills our spirits to overflowing. It is when we study the Bible that we hear God speak to our hearts. We are His servants and His soldiers, and we need our orders for that day. We need to talk to God about our needs and the needs of our family members and our friends. We need to get ourselves clothed in the whole armor of God before we go out to face the world that is so anti-God and anti-His purposes.

The majority of Christians have time to read just about anything that is of particular interest to them. But when it comes to reading in order to study the Bible, they claim that they just don't have the time or that they can't understand it. The Bible says that if we are Christians and have the Holy Spirit in our lives, one of the primary ministries of the Spirit is to teach us and to lead us into truth, and the truth will set us free. Now that promise is not given to clergymen alone. It is for all of us. We will not get all that we need by listening to sermons and Bible studies here and there. We need to search for these truths personally. Then they will hide in our hearts so that we might not sin against God so easily. They will also be there to comfort us and for us to share with others when the need arises. But you still have a hard time getting God's people to study His Word.

The third tool is suffering. Paul said that what he wanted most in his life was to know Jesus Christ, and the power of His resurrection and the fellowship of His sufferings. Now if the truth were known, most of us would get busy praying and studying if we could just avoid the suffering part. But one thing I've learned is that when I see a Christian who Jesus just shines through, I know that when I talk to them, I will discover that they have been through some fire, and having been tested, they have come out pure gold. They know what it means to have suffered, and in that pain, they have looked unto Jesus. They have found in His throne room the grace to meet all of their needs. And their spirits sing in the midst of the fire. This is Hilda Waddell.

Hilda was born in 1913 in Brownsville, located in west Tennessee. As she shared those early years with me, you could sense her deep respect for her parents.

"Father," she said, "was a very godly man. He had a good bit of land and a number of people who helped him work the farm. Father read the Bible to his family daily. It was also his custom to get up at two or three o'clock in the morning to pray."

The children were home schooled by their mother. Part of the education included studying the Bible. Hilda's memories of her home were God-honoring.

In 1925, during a tent revival, the Holy Spirit reached down and touched Hilda's heart, convicting her of her sin and of her need for Jesus Christ. She remembers vividly that day when she asked Jesus to forgive her of her sins and to come into her heart and save her soul. The recollection of her emotions showed in her countenance as she told me about skipping along the road afterward, wanting to shout about her new joy in being set free.

Some years passed, and Hilda became a schoolteacher. As often happens, along came a handsome young man who swept her off her feet. They soon decided that they wanted to get married. Knowing that Father would not give his blessing, they chose to elope. On the trip to West Memphis, Arkansas,

Hilda shared that the Holy Spirit tried to stop this wedding. She refused to listen and continued to follow her feelings instead of her convictions.

Great detail is not necessary here except to say that this immature, self-centered man made her life miserable. His infidelity eventually drove her to feel that she had no alternative but to leave him and return to her "Father's" home. She did not go back alone. By now she had two little children.

There were people who worked for them who were able to take care of the children so that Hilda could pursue her career in teaching. There was one problem. At that time, teachers were better able to get a job if they were single. A position came open in a school close by. Hilda was told that if she got a divorce, the job would easily be hers. Tears still ran down her cheeks as she told me how devastated she was over even the thought of divorce. However, it seemed that she had no choice since there was no chance of the marriage succeeding. She got the divorce, and the job was hers.

The first child was a little girl named Jan. The second was a little boy name Johnny. Both were healthy little children until one day when Jan got very sick. This was in 1934. The diagnosis was encephalitis. The illness left this little girl in a vegetative state and in need of constant care. Jan never grew like a normal child would. Hilda was advised to put her into an institution, but there was no way that she could make herself take that advice. Because there was help in their home and from friends through the years, Hilda was able to teach and even travel if she should need to. Jan eventually simply curled up into a fetal position, her body very stiff. They had a sun porch with a specially designed place for Jan to rest. There was nothing more that they could have done for her.

Hilda's family recall got a little complicated about this point, but I'll try to get this right. Hilda's father was married before he married Hilda's mother. His first wife died. This wife's daughter married a Dr. Waddell who had a son named Oswell Waddell. Oswell now enters Hilda's story. He loved Hilda long before she knew anything about it. After seeing him demonstrate his love with great sensitivity, Hilda was able to believe that she could trust him and could indeed love him. They married and moved Hilda, Jan and Johnny to Rogersville, Alabama. God blessed Hilda and Oswell with three more children, Ramsey, Mary Lou, and Jesse (Bo).

When Hilda was saved back in 1925, she had a very clear impression that God said to her, "*Study the Bible.*" Her father being her role model, she always got up at two-thirty or three o'clock in the morning to pray and listen to the Lord for instruction and to read the Bible. One morning, she heard with spirit ears the Lord say to her, "*Stay in the word to keep from worrying.*" This was after her children had married and had their own families. It seemed that in her family were so many needs of all sorts. Her heart longed for all the ones she loved so much to come to Jesus and find the rest that they needed. She found herself worrying instead of resting in Jesus.

Hilda's response to God that morning was a turning point in her spiritual walk. She said, "Lord, whatever it takes ...I give all my children and grandchildren to you. I won't worry! I won't question! I won't doubt!"

She heard God clearly answer in her spirit ears, "Hilda, I can take care of all your burdens!" *She was free!*

Shortly after this, her son Bo called and told her that his wife, Rosalind, had been diagnosed with Hodgkin's disease. Hilda recalled calmly saying, "Bo, put it in the Lord's hands." God did take care of Bo's family. Through many difficult circumstances, their family came to the place of full surrender of their individual lives and their home to the Lordship of Jesus Christ. They all serve Him faithfully through their church.

Johnny's story brought the most pain to Hilda's heart. She told me what a responsible man he grew up to be. He served with honor in the military service. At some point, he found himself in a major crisis period. He turned to alcohol instead of to the Lord. Alcoholism almost destroyed him. I'll just zero in on one experience. Johnny came to Hilda's home and went berserk. They had to call the police for help. Johnny was admitted to a treatment center for the intense help that he desperately needed. He was out of control!

God worked a miracle in Johnny's life. Finding himself at the bottom, there was no place to look but up. Johnny reached out to God for the deliverance that he needed. God saved his soul! Such grace! Such mercy! What an awesome God Johnny came to know by experience that day. Now he found himself hungering for the Word of God. Hilda described her son as having such a sweet, generous spirit.

Hilda then told me about her daughter Ramsey and her husband Dwight Plott. I don't want to go into details here because there will be a chapter about the Plott family. But let me say that Hilda was praying for Dwight's salvation. He was a doctor whose life was filled with all sorts of successful things. But he had no understanding of the most important thing of all, a personal relationship with Jesus Christ. Let me just say here that

Dwight was gloriously saved during a revival. His life was completely turned around. What a testimony he bore the last years of his life.

One by one, God worked bringing Hilda's children and grandchildren to salvation. One grandson she said she believed was saved but so far outside of God's will for his life. She prayed for him diligently and fervently. He took his own life.

There was something I could not help but sense; Hilda loves each and every one of her family members. She knows how to "bless" them.

I asked her what her favorite verse of scripture was. She hesitated, as if to have to single out one when she loved it all was almost too difficult. However, she did share one.

> "Trust in the Lord with all your heart,
> And do not lean on your own understanding.
> In all your ways acknowledge Him,
> And He will make your paths straight."
>
> -Proverbs 3:5–6 (NAS)

Hilda shared some real wisdom she had gained through experience. Wait until you hear from God. If you don't, don't do it. She also shared with me that as God looks at us, everything that doesn't look like Christ has to be sanded off. I remember hearing Manley Beasley, a preacher with such depth when it came to understanding faith and how it works in our lives, calling this God's work of applying Heavenly sandpaper. Sometimes things in our lives that do not honor our Father in Heaven must have course sandpaper applied. Other times our rough places are not as bad and require medium sandpaper. There are still other times when we are walking close to Jesus that we may just need fine finishing sandpaper to help us shine even more for our Lord. I think Hilda was thinking of this when she spoke of the need for everything that doesn't look like Jesus to be sanded off.

Hilda has written many poems through the years. Ramsey has put her collection together to share with all her family and many friends. I have chosen a few of these for your enrichment.

December 15, 1975

Lord, that night when my soul was so torn,
Concerning the salvation and service of my own,
I said, "Whatever it takes to get them saved and in Your will,
Let it happen – I won't worry or question or doubt."
I had no idea what lay ahead,
When I made such a statement as that,
You called my hand with situations which
Could easily make me doubt.
But faithful You are to me, and to them,
I have not broken my word,
But I've prayed night and day many times,
And there is always evidence You've heard.
You've held me in a way not my own:
Aware of Your strength and grace,
And regardless of what I found,
You, too, were with me in that place.
The years have passed since 1975,
And one by one they've come
To give themselves to You afresh,
Or to receive You as their Lord,
These glorious decisions were mountain peaks,
And in spite of dark days I've had

There's more to keep my heart fixed on You,
And praising from a heart that's glad.

ME

I am a piece of marble - hard,
Defiant of the Sculptor's hand:
Each chip requires a labor of the One
Who seeks to make me something grand,
And flaws are many, everywhere!
I wonder why He ever chose to use
Me as a piece of His display.
It will mean long hours of patience
On the Sculptor's part.
It will mean a making over of my heart.
But He is patient, time no problem
In His plan.
My God, my God! How great Thou art!
In His own time He'll make of me
That which His heart began.

October 25, 1975

MY TEARS

My tears are precious in Your sight,
For I lie weeping on your breast.
This desert in my life I make a well with tears.
(Psalm 84:6)
They even seem to strengthen and give rest.
Like a child of mine who comes to me when hurt
I clasp him in my arms and comfort

His tears and sobbing heart. My heart does break.
I add my strength to his; of his hurt become a part.
So do You to me in this strange land,
As child of Yours, I journey through.
Down here there is nothing really precious to my heart
But the great joys that come from fellowship with You.

December 5, 1981

ONE ANSWER

I could not know why trouble came to me,
And trembling soul of mine was sore disarmed,
Until I sat with one with whom sad trouble dwelt,
And though she trembled, I was calm,
I had already sailed through such a sea,
And knew its rocky shore and wave;
My eye had pierced beyond the storm,
And lashed my breaking ship to One who'd save,
Who knows but that your trying hour,
With sorrow as a deep abyss,
Was meant for you to learn to lead another trembling soul
Through such a time as this!
II Corinthians 1:4

5. *Preparation for Battle*

Ramsey Plott Williams

In a previous chapter I shared with you the testimony of Hilda Waddell. Hilda is the mother of my dear friend, Ramsey Plott Williams. Now I would like to tell you something about Ramsey's story. Not the whole story, because that would take a book of its own. The emphasis here will be on one particular event in the Plott family's life.

However, you do need a little information that will help you understand how the Lord has worked in Ramsey's life. She was raised in a home with a godly mother seeing that her children were in church from the beginning of their lives. She saw her mother diligently studying the Bible, serving in the church, teaching, ministering to others in the community tirelessly.

This kind of testimony plus the boundaries that are placed around the children as to what they are and are not allowed to do can often be a really irritating experience. The adjective the children found that best described their mother was "fanatic."

Ramsey was a free spirit. Still a teenager, she fell in love with Dwight Plott. Dwight's family went to a church that believed just the opposite of what the Baptist doctrines taught. In spite of this difference, Ramsey saw in Dwight many things to be admired. He was very intelligent. He knew what he wanted to be, a doctor. He set his goals and was tenacious in going after the prize. Ramsey admired this and ignored the fact that nowhere in his plans did he consider he needed God to help him achieve his degrees.

After they married, Ramsey knew that she was to be submissive to her husband. Dwight had no desire to go to church, and so Ramsey did not go under the guise of submission. Dwight was the center of her security. She really didn't feel that big a need for God now. In her rationalization, her relationship to Dwight was her excuse for not having a right relationship with God.

It did not take long for this rebellion to take a toll on Ramsey. She had no peace, and that presented a problem for her because her own inner turmoil began to manifest itself in her attitude toward Dwight. The marriage was in trouble. Feelings of coldness and deadness were more evident than intimate and caring moments. The marriage had disintegrated to the point of each one feeling that they should just go their separate ways and do their own things.

Spiritual warfare was so intense that Ramsey went into her

bedroom one day deeply depressed. She fell on the floor asking God to forgive her for playing Christian since she was nine years old. She needed God's forgiveness for ridiculing her mother, the fanatic, and for placing her security and faith in Dwight instead of God.

That day she made a conscious choice to accept the Bible as truth whether she understood it all or not. That was the time that the Bible came alive to her. From then on, she could not get enough study. God then took her into a very effective teaching ministry not only through the church, but also in smaller neighborhood study groups. Doors opened for her to go to many different places to share the testimony as to the forgiveness and faithfulness of her God.

Ramsey was born again in February of 1978. Even after genuine conversion, there came another time of going through some bad depression. Her new commitment to God was personal and did not change Dwight one bit. Now there was an unequally yoked marriage, and Ramsey was the fanatic. Dwight continued to do his own thing. His career, golf, restoring cars, University of Alabama football, his two prized Rolls Royce's, and other things were all-consuming. He needed no one, especially God.

Ramsey decided to go back to college and complete the work necessary to get her degree. With the academic load, her family to take care of, a house to keep, responsibilities at church and so much more, she found herself overwhelmed and fatigued all the time. The depression reached the place of almost convincing her that suicide was the only way to get free.

Let me interject something at this point. Dwight and Ramsey had three sons. Dwight was very proud of his boys, but Ramsey has that kind of love that just demonstrates itself so freely. These children always knew how loved they were. So for her to even consider leaving them shows how desperate she was.

Perry and Marilyn Calvert were very close friends of the Plotts. Perry and Ramsey had gone to high school together in Rogersville, Alabama. They knew of Ramsey's despondency. Marilyn sent Ramsey to Bro. Jimmy Jackson at Whitesburg Baptist Church. The Plotts were members of a local Methodist church at that time. Bro. Jimmy asked Ramsey a question that made sense to her, "Are you being fed spiritually?" It did not take her long to know that the answer was no. She then started attending Whitesburg.

I believe that this was about the time I met Ramsey. Marilyn called me one day and asked if I would have lunch with Ramsey and see if I could help her work through some of the problems that still were very real. We met at Quincy's. We were the first ones there, and we were the last ones to leave. Ramsey was very open and extremely broken. This was the beginning of a friendship that I treasure.

Many people began to pray for Dwight's salvation. Several men played golf with him on a regular basis. But when it came to times where spiritual matters came up, he was cold and indifferent to any suggestion that he needed God. It did reach a point where, when Ramsey and the boys went to church, Dwight would stay home and read the scriptures. One by one, Charlie, Mickey and William accepted Jesus Christ as their personal Savior. Dwight would come to see them baptized, but that was all the church attendance.

Whitesburg had a revival with Dr. Jess Henley preaching on prophecy. No one had a better understanding of this subject. On Friday night, Dwight went to the service. Mickey made his profession of faith that night. Conviction was so powerful on Dwight that his suit coat was dripping wet. My personal memory of that night was that I was praying for him during the invitation and suddenly felt a chill go through my body that was gripping. I knew Satan was working to stop people from praying.

Bro. Jimmy had an opportunity to talk to Dwight. Without body slamming him, which would not have worked, he simply stated, "I came to you one day with back problems. You recommended Dr. Haws for me. Yours is a spiritual problem, and I recommend Jesus Christ to you." This was in February of 1979. When you plant seeds, you wait quite a long time more often than not for visual evidence that the germination took place and something is indeed growing. There were many caring friends who shared with him when there was an opening but did not push him.

The last week in October of 1979, Dwight and Ramsey were on their way to an Alabama football game. Dwight told Ramsey to drive. He opened his Bible and began reading at Matthew 1:1 and read for three hours. Nothing was said. Just silence.

The following Sunday night, Mickey was baptized. Of course, Dwight was there. During the invitation he turned to Ramsey and said that he was ready to go. He asked her if she wanted to go with him. He emphatically told her that he was not doing this for her. He gave his heart and life to Jesus Christ that night, and it was the beginning of a new life. This was in November of 1979. He was baptized this time for the right reason. It was a testimony stating that he was buried with Christ in baptism and raised to walk in newness of life.

The manifestations of this new man were so powerfully evident. He read the Bible constantly, reading it from cover to cover. He became a prayer warrior. He was an avid soul winner. He joined the choir. He didn't have a great singing gift, but he loved singing praises to his Lord. He went to Israel to experience the land of Jesus' earthly life. He was a visionary, believing that God was going to do something awesome at Whitesburg and that there was a need to purchase property to build on. He was a cheerful giver. When we had a building fund emphasis, his pledge was $100,000. I'm sure he would not want me to include this, but since he's in Heaven now, and I'm at the computer, I think I'll do it anyhow. He sold his two treasured Rolls Royce's and gave the money to this fund.

Several different people told me about the changed Dr. Plott. They said he was the meanest acting doctor until he was saved. Then he became the sweetest and most caring physician. It was not unusual for him to go into a room to wash his hands, and you could hear him singing something like *Amazing Grace.*

In January of 1984, Dwight was having some unusual symptoms that led him to the tests that revealed that he had a brain tumor. Since he was a neurologist, he knew the symptoms and could read the tests results as well as anyone. He simply stated that he had six months to live.

Prior to this, Ramsey remembered that from August 8 until November, 6, 1983, she had felt sensations that she described as oppressive. They were like anxiety attacks that seemed to be centered on Dwight. Psalm 139, Philippians 4:3–9, II Timothy 1:12 and Romans 8:27–29 were some verses that she read over and over for comfort. Dwight's symptoms began in October of 1983. Weakness developed on one side. There was loss of balance and fatigue. He missed the Auburn/Alabama game that fall, which made everyone know that he was in trouble. The cancer progressed steadily. The CAT scan was done after Christmas. Inoperable. No cure. He refused radiation because he knew it would not help but would take away the quality of life for the little time that was left. His office was close to the hospital. He walked there and had a talk with Ramsey. They agreed to five things they would pray for:

1. That God's will would be done and not theirs.

2. That people would see a power in them that was not their own.

3. That they would be able to share Christ with others through this crisis.

4. That there would be no bitterness in them or in their sons.

5. That God would be merciful.

The decision was made that he would live until he died. They agreed that they would talk about their circumstances and if they needed to, they would cry.

Dwight made an appointment to meet with Bro. Dick Thomassian, the Minister of Music at Whitesburg Baptist Church. He arranged to have a tape made concerning the things that were on his mind. He wanted this tape to be played at his Memorial Service.

His work schedule was limited from that point on. His expertise in his field of medicine was still very valuable to his colleagues.

He was in church up until two weeks before he died. The Sunday morning before he died on Monday, his Sunday school class all went over to his bedside and had their Bible study in his room. In spite of the fact that Dwight became totally dependent on those around him, there was not a sign of bitterness toward God. He would always say, "God can still do whatever He wants to do."

I personally had carefully observed this family as they were guided by the Holy Spirit through these six months. I marveled at their courage and their consistent faithfulness in the midst of the fire. I asked Ramsey to share with me some of the secrets of such victory. Here are some of her answers.

They focused on the things they had to be thankful for. (I call this proper placement of your magnifying glass ...on the positives and not on the negatives.)

Because the paralysis started in the toes, Dwight needed help putting his shoes on. Something like this reminded Ramsey of how thankful she was for a healthy body. So she would start each day on her knees getting prepared to help someone else in their weakness.

They recognized soon that roles were reversed. Dwight had been the one charged with taking care of his family. Now Charlie, Mickey and William became caretakers.

From the beginning until the end, they would read the Bible aloud daily, saturating their minds with God's truths. The radio was on much of the time so that Dwight could listen to two of his favorite Bible teachers, Charles Swindoll and J. Vernon Magee. A little book entitled *Precious Bible Promises* made the nights easier. Some nights he would feel like if he went to sleep that he would stop breathing. As Ramsey read these promises, he would fall asleep. No one in the family had anxiety about death. Dwight had expressed many times how ready he was to see Jesus. "I've fallen in love with Him, and I can't wait to see Him face to face," was his sincere desire.

It was July 2, 1984, and Whitesburg was right in the middle of the *I Love America* celebration with the living flag. Dwight had been one of the people who proudly sang from this awesome structure. But this time his spot would be filled by someone else. This was the day that he would celebrate something much more magnificent and wonderful than the Fourth of July. This would be his ultimate Independence Day. This would be the day he would be set free from this frail diseased body and be totally delivered from all limitations. This would be the day he longed for. He would see Jesus face to face.

Ramsey called me that evening and asked if I was going to the church that night. I said I was not. I had been at the Plott's most of the day and decided that I would stay at home. She asked if she could come and pick me up and if I could spend some time with her that evening. I was only too happy to be there for her. When we got to her house, I found out that she had not eaten. I got her to sit down and eat a little something. While we were at the table, William came in and with the sweetest, calmest manner said, "I think Daddy has gone to be with Jesus." He had been in the bed with his father at the time. Someone was always right there with Dwight. We went to the bedroom, and he had indeed very quietly exited his physical body, and as the Bible says, "We are confident, yes, well pleased rather to be absent from the body and to be present with the Lord" (II Corinthians 5:8 NKJV).

There were several people in the room: Charlie, Mickey, William, Charlie Goldman (Ramsey's nephew), Greg Ray, Rusty Martin, Dave Berryhill, Terry Herald, Dana Calvert Hobbs, Rita and Ramsey. There was no hysteria, just peace. There was no confusion, just joy. I remember how everyone went from one to the other and just embraced one another. I recall Rusty saying that he would like to lead us in prayer. Ramsey expressed to him that she would like to be the one to pray. She knelt down by the bed, put her arms across Dwight's lifeless body and prayed the most beautiful prayer you can imagine. She praised God. She thanked him for saving all her family. But she thanked Him especially for saving Dwight and giving her sons a Christian father for four years. She thanked him for the influence Dwight had on so many people. It was something I probably will never forget. She got up, and it seemed that little praise songs began to fill the room. All of us were singing together on Tannahill Circle while Dwight was singing and praising God in Heaven.

We went into the den and were talking and rejoicing when it occurred to Ramsey that she had not called anyone to come and pronounce him dead and make arrangements to pick up his body. Hugh Bell, a longtime friend and co-worker, was called.

The outpouring of love that was spilled out on their family in the days that followed was awesome. But the Memorial Service for Dwight was one for the books. Bro. Jimmy got up before the huge crowd that had come to pay their respects. He said that this might be a first, but that Dwight had made a tape when he found out that he had a limited time to live. His request was that this tape be played at this service. And so it was.

It went something like this: "Hello from Heaven." That got everyone's attention. Then he proceeded to tell about how he had prayed for most of the people gathered there. He wanted one last chance to beg them to take another look at their priorities. He said that he had learned late in his life (he was forty-nine when he died) that nothing really matters but Jesus and what each of us has decided to do with Him. If your life is spent getting to the top of your career ladder, accumulating great wealth and tons of material things, and if you have spent your leisure time on a golf course or some other sport or activity, and you have neglected Jesus, you have missed the most important thing in life. And when you die, the only thing that will matter is what you did with Jesus. The testimony was powerful, and later Ramsey was told of several people who came to know Jesus Christ in a personal, life changing way that day. Dwight went on then to sing to us *Amazing Grace.*

Dwight was not there physically in their home, but Jesus Christ kept His promise, "I will never leave you nor forsake you." And He never will. He has been faithful to take care of their needs. Ramsey has continued to grow in her relationship with God. She is still faithfully serving through the spiritual gifts that God has given her. She reaches out to share with and help so many people in so many ways.

Several years passed, and God brought Phil Williams into her life. After becoming friends and helping each other through a very difficult set of circumstances, the friendship grew into love. They were married, and God has blessed them in so many ways. Ramsey's boys love Phil, and Phil's sons love Ramsey. The sons have married and are blessing Ramsey with many grandchildren. Both Phil and Ramsey adore children, and so they are the classic grandparents, doting on each one of these children.

I have expressed to Ramsey and to many others how thankful I am that God permitted me to witness the way He was honored through the trial and the testimony of the Plott family. I know that this will encourage many of you who read this just as it has continued to encourage and strengthen my own faith.

6. *Circumstances As Seen Through Jesus*

" Now may the Lord of peace himself give you peace at all times and in every way."
2 Thessalonians 3:16

The Trents

The story comes to my mind of a group of war refugees who had been uprooted from their homes and families, endured great suffering and losing everything. Their lives were so inspiring. Everyone around noticed that the Christians among them continually gave thanks to God. When we see people going through such pain, our instinct is to find a way to get them out of their circumstances. Very seldom do we stop to think that their situations are the very tools God is using to grow them into victorious conquerors in the midst of the fire. God does not always deliver us from our trials. But He always promises to be in the trial with us. His is the light that shines from within in the darkest of days.

This brings me to the one I would like to introduce to you in this chapter. Her name is Annette Trent, and she is from Athens, Alabama. One day Ramsey Williams suggested that I might think about talking to her and including her family's story in this book. She arranged for us to meet at her house for lunch. It was a most rewarding experience.

Like so many of the other stories I've shared with you, Annette was raised in a Christian home. Good moral teaching was a given. Her parents took their children to church regularly. Annette gives credit and thanks to many good Sunday school teachers and Girl's Auxiliary leaders for their encouragement and their willingness to be godly role models.

When Annette was just eight years old, her mother died after surgery. She was only thirty-three years old. Her father was about forty at the time. He found himself with the awesome responsibility of suddenly becoming a mother and father to their only child.

At age ten, little Annette professed her faith in Jesus Christ. It was not until she was fourteen years old that she understood what it meant to respond to the convicting power of the Holy Spirit leading her to totally surrender all that she was to God. She wasn't sure exactly what God would expect her to do, (maybe even go to Africa, snakes and all) but as intimidating as that was, she was still willing to do whatever He asked her to do. One of the blessings God had for her was a wonderful husband, Robert Trent. The two of them together, plus God in control, made an unbeatable team.

After Annette graduated from Howard College, (now it is Samford University) and completed her work for her Bachelor of Music degree, she got the surprise of her life. She was asked to take the position of college professor on the Music faculty at Athens State College. She later received her Master's degree at the University of North Alabama. There she was in the middle of all the doctors. The old inferiority complex quickly raised its ugly head. Although she knew only God could have opened this door for her, she felt grossly inadequate for the task. "Lord, if I'm not supposed to be here, show me and I'll leave, but if I am supposed to be here, give me the assurance of your presence and power." This was her prayer. I don't have to tell you that she continued in that position throughout her career. Her peers and her students held her in the highest regard.

God blessed Robert and Annette with two beautiful children. They raised them in a home filled with love and taught them about the things of God, gently guiding them to Jesus Christ. The truth is that this does not automatically mean that children are going to be delivered from exercising their free will and deciding to go their own way. This is the greatest testing for Christian parents. Annette recalled hearing in her spirit God saying to her, "Okay, you made an A in the lecture; let's see how you do in the lab."

Their son Steve and his testimony are what I would like to zero in on. His rebellion had taken him as far away from his early teachings as you can get. While he was in college, twenty-one years old, he had been with some friends to a concert. Asleep in the back seat, almost home, at two o'clock in the morning, there was a car accident. Alcohol had been a part of their good time. Six miles from home at a place called French's Mill, the driver of the car fell asleep. The car hit a culvert. Steve was thrown out the hatchback, and his neck was broken. Before the dust had settled, a game warden who was waiting to transport a prisoner to Florence, Alabama, came by the scene of the accident. He had a radio and called for help. He saw that Steve was still alive and covered him and waited for help to arrive.

In the middle of the night, that dreaded ring pierced the darkness.

Annette answered the phone and heard the patrolman say, "Mrs. Trent, Steve wanted me to call you. There's been an accident."

"How bad is it?"

He replied that he just did not know. They rushed to the Athens Limestone Emergency Room. She told the attending physician that she wanted Dr. Frank Haws to be his doctor. (Do you believe that it was an accident that Dr. Haws was on call that night?) Of course not! The Trents were beginning to see God at work in the midst of this fiery trial.

Steve was taken to Athens, and from there he was transferred to Huntsville Hospital. The diagnosis was a broken neck. The next words were your worst nightmare; paralyzed from the chest down. Complications plagued Steve, making his recovery time take eleven months of hospitalization and rehabilitation. The question was asked, "Why did God do this to me?" God didn't do this to be mean to Steve. The truth is that God is too loving to be mean and too wise to make a mistake. God permitted this knowing full well that what would ultimately come out of it would one day produce in Steve a deep faith that would bring glory to his Father's Name. He would learn this the hard way, as many of us have had to do.

Circumstances like these have destroyed many people. It was for Steve a new beginning place. When he recovered enough, he continued his education, got two degrees and got a good job. Robert and Annette had prayed that God would bring a godly woman into Steve's life. And that is where Diana comes into the story. No one doubted that she was an answer to their prayers. She not only loved Steve deeply but also was qualified to give him the specific care that he needed. Steve was thirty-five when they married. Things could not have worked out better for them.

On December1, 1995, Steve and Diana were traveling home from Birmingham, Alabama. They had a van that had been designed to meet Steve's physical needs. Again they were almost home. Annette had gone to meet Robert in Huntsville. A sudden fear overwhelmed her, causing her to pray urgently. She later found out that this was almost the precise time that a second accident happened. A man in a pickup truck hit the van from the rear right side, knocking it into a tree. Two or three minutes before it happened, Diana had moved to the back just behind Steve. The impact was on the side where Diana had been sitting just minutes before. The force of the seat belt broke her back, also tearing the abdominal muscles that hold in your vital organs, broke her ankle, punctured a lung and more, leaving her slowly bleeding to death.

The force of the seat belt caused Steve's liver to be knocked off the ligament that holds it in place. Profuse internal bleeding was maybe the most life threatening problem. They quit counting at twenty units of blood for each one of them after they got to the hospital. He had a broken pelvis, broken femur, broken ribs and punctured lungs.

Once again a cell phone was right there. The driver of the car behind them called for an ambulance immediately. Two med techs from Nashville were on their way to Wheeler Lodge and had "somehow" missed two exits. They took the exit that brought them right to Steve and Diana and pulled over and offered their help. Anyone who knows the Lord knows that this was no accident. After their "God-sent" ministry was through, they just turned around and went back to Nashville. Steve and Diana were taken to Decatur General Hospital. Diana was transferred to Huntsville Hospital the next day for surgery. When Steve was on his way to surgery, he asked if he could have a minute with his parents. A sweet time of prayer met a need in each of their lives. They were thankful to God for all the evidences of His Holy presence.

Many surgeries later, Steve and Diana were released from the hospital and were taken to Robert and Annette's home to recuperate. As co-caretakers, they realized more than ever before just how wonderfully God can melt your hearts together when your focus is on Him and your heart and hands and feet are privileged to care for your children. There they experienced again the truth in God's Word, "I can do all things through Christ who strengthens me" (Philippians 4:13 (NAS).

You may be asking why God would allow so much to come into a person's life. Before we go on further, please let me share something with you that has been such a blessing to me for many years and through many trials. In II Corinthians 1:3–4 (NAS), Paul, the apostle of Jesus Christ, says:

> "Blessed be the God and Father of our Lord Jesus Christ, the Father of all mercies and God of all comfort; who comforts us in all our affliction so that we may be able to comfort those who are in any affliction with the comfort with which we ourselves are comforted by God."

The Trents understand this as a result of experience. Steve, Diana and the Trents have had many opportunities to share their testimony of God's love and faithfulness with other hurting and lost people. Steve is able to teach a Sunday school class, not just out of head knowledge, but out of soul experiences, and is an ordained deacon in his church.

Then in II Corinthians 1:9–10 (NAS), he says:

"Indeed we had the sentence of death within ourselves in order that we should not trust in ourselves, but in God who raises the dead, who delivered us from so great a peril of death and will deliver us, He on whom we set our hope. And He will yet deliver us."

There is no doubt in my mind that Steve and Diana live in the resurrection power of God and not in their fleshly abilities. And you see, I have never personally met Steve and Diana.

The third reason I believe God permits suffering in His children's lives is found in the eleventh verse of this same first chapter:

"You also joining in helping us through your prayers, that thanks may be given by many persons on our behalf for the favor bestowed upon us through the prayers of many."

Fiery trials draw the extended body of Christ together in one Spirit. Although I did not know the Trents at that time, I did know Annette's two cousins who are members of the same church I attend. They were so devastated over Steve and Diana's situation; they even reached out and gave me the privilege of hearing about the need so that I could join so many others in so many different places lifting this precious family up to the throne room of grace. It blessed all of us when we heard the good news that after nine months of God's tender loving care, they were able to go back to their own home. Steve is self-employed and still filled with praise and thanksgiving to God. Annette compared their situation to an eagle that flies directly into the storm. The thermals (air currents) lift his wings, and he is able to soar above the storm rather than beneath it and not be crushed under its power. She was full of quotes that afternoon. This is her favorite poem

> *Two men looking through bars*
> *One saw the mud, the other saw stars.*

Someone said to Annette one day, "When it rains, it storms."

"Yes," she replied, "but I have a great umbrella."

I asked her to share with us her favorite verse of scripture. It is Deuteronomy 33:27a.

"The Eternal God is thy refuge, and underneath are the everlasting arms." (nas)

Add to that the comfort found in Isaiah 40:29–31.(NAS)

> *He gives strength to the weary,*
> *and to him who lacks might he increases power,*
> *though youths grow weary and tired,*
> *and vigorous young men stumble badly,*
> *yet those who wait for the lord*
> *Will gain new strength;*
> *they will mount up with wings like eagles,*
> *they will run and not get tired,*
> *they will walk and not become weary.*

The Trents are great examples of what God means when He says that we are more than conquerors. Instead of choosing to feel so sorry for themselves, they determined that they would commit themselves to being so focused on God that they would not miss out on anything He was doing in their lives. As Annette shared their story, silent tears would surface from time to time. But then she would burst into praise! She plays the piano so beautifully and sings from her spirit to her Lord.

She shared some of the praise and worship songs that the Holy Spirit is producing in her. No doubt we will all be singing these some day soon.

Thank you, Ramsey, for making this visit possible. And thank you, Annette, for encouraging us to never give up, but to always remember to keep looking Heavenward! God is indeed faithful, so real and personal and ever present!

7. *Faith, Not Worry*
–My Choice

Barbara Causey

The story I am going to share with you in this chapter is very special to me. This is a bit of Barbara Woods Causey's testimony. I know this one a little more personally. I lived through these rough times with her. She is my little sister.

If you have read my childhood memories book, *Sweet Peas, Lizards and Walnut Street,* you may remember her as being the little blonde haired, blue-eyed beauty. Everyone in the family protected her. As she grew up, somehow we must have conveyed to her that she was unable to be independent. We continued to make her decisions for her after she became a teenager. Somewhere along the way she began to feel like she was a little deficient in the brain department. Now this was absolutely untrue. But if you never have the opportunity to think for yourself, you can assume just such a mistaken idea. And you begin to act as if this is true.

Barbara met a young man from a neighboring town while she was a freshman in college. His name was Sonny Norton. Sonny was a really "cool" character. He played football. He was very popular. He was a "take charge" personality. This was of course what Barbara was used to. They fell madly in love. Over the strong objections of our parents, she finally exerted some independence, and declared she was indeed going to marry him.

The marriage was dysfunctional from the beginning. Sonny came from a home where his father, an alcoholic, deserted his family. Mrs. Norton was left to raise three children on a minimal salary working at a laundry. Because of her circumstances, she was extremely bitter. Because Sonny never received the blessing from his parents that God intends for all of us to have, he had no way of knowing how to be a blessing to his wife, and later on to his children. He had dreams of hitting pay dirt one day and experiencing affluence. That never happened.

The beautiful thing that came out of their marriage was that they had a beautiful daughter and then a precious son. Because Sonny had no father role model, he had very little understanding of how to bless his children in a godly way.

When he was thirty years old, he dove off into shallow water and fractured his neck. Shortly after this, doctors discovered that he had a rare cancer for someone his age. They gave him six months to live.

Barbara was faced with a mountain that was so overwhelming that there was nothing inside her that prepared her to be able to cope with these circumstances. Her mind hid in a state of shock. She described it as being in a deep well. She could hear voices and was aware that there were people around her, but she could not respond with any clarity.

Barbara worked for a law firm. Fortunately, the lawyers loved her, as everybody did, and were very sympathetic and understanding of the condition that she was in. She spent most of her time in the bathroom at the office just crying her heart out.

I remember getting a call from Mother one day asking me if I could come to Jackson and see if I could get through to her. I had become a Christian just a year or so before this happened. From the minute Jesus Christ came into my life, I was such a different person that Mother thought if anyone could reach her, it might be me. I had devoured everything I could get my hands on that would teach me more about Jesus. I didn't know much, but what I did know was that Jesus could help Barbara even if none of us could. I rode a bus from Mobile, Alabama, to Jackson, Mississippi. I remember going in to see Barbara in her bedroom. She had the blankest look in her eyes. She was there physically, but not mentally, emotionally or spiritually. I talked my heart out, but it seemed to do no good.

I don't know how long it was, but it was Jesus who finally reached her. She was in the bathroom looking into a mirror one day. She could feel herself loosing control of the last bit of sanity. She heard bells ringing. Knowing there were no bells in the house, she had a moment of clarity where she realized that she had to do something then or it was going to be too late. She asked herself what other people did when they were in such crisis. The thought came to her mind that they probably prayed. She cried out to God and told him that she couldn't go through this alone. She had a husband who was dying. She had two little children. They had no insurance. There was not enough income to live on. She needed God to take over her life. A peace came into her that delivered her from the shock and depression that had immobilized her.

Now for the first time in her twenty-eight years, she felt empowered from within. There was so much to go through, but she would not have to handle it alone. Sonny lived two and a half years and died when he was thirty-three.

During those two and a half years, they saw God take care of their needs. One example will suffice. Barbara was driving home from work one day. She knew the kitchen pantry was empty. She said, "God, there is nothing for my family to eat except some rice and butter. I know You are not going to let us go without food. I trust You to provide for us." When she got home, they had a lady who took care of Sonny while Barbara was at work. She had seen that there was practically no food. She had noticed that the freezer was in desperate need of defrosting. As she began to thaw the clump of ice that had formed, she noticed something under the ice. It was a duck! She thawed it, put it in the oven and baked it. When Barbara walked in, she smelled meat. Duck and rice and butter! God had heard her and had already hidden that duck for just such an occasion as this. There were so many more stories of His provision just as awesome. He was building her faith for the days ahead.

Their pastor, Bro. Sam Mason, was a Godsend to them. He was there through the illness. He was there for Barbara and the children in the weeks and months and years that followed. He had a shepherd's heart and knew how to tend the sheep.

During the time that Barbara was so despondent, God gave

me a poem that expressed my deep concern for her. I would like to share it with you.

TO A ROSE

I came upon one of God's loveliest creations . . .
A sweet, fragile, yet so beautiful rose.
In youth's innocence it stood in glowing grace;
Its bud sheltered from life's bitter blows.
It opened with its head held high in the air
And was looked upon and admired by all around.
Til one day came the tortuous winds and rains
Destined to crush and beat the rose to the ground.
The rains they came as I knew they would
And pierced the thorns into the stately stem.
The tears from the rain trickled down the green leaves,
And I wept as I saw my rose growing dim.
Then I said, "Little rose, the rains will cease.
After this storm, there'll be a calm.
The sun will shine and give you new birth,
And the beauty of life will return.
Again you will glow in the warmth of the sun;
Stand erect with a smile on your face.
For the God who has made you loves you still,
And will show you a new peaceful place."

Rita Coker

After Sonny's death, Barbara focused her attention on raising her children alone. She had no desire to marry again. However, there were some friends who felt the need to match her up with a nice man. They arranged a date with Will Causey. Will's wife had died in a tragic automobile accident. Because his wife's family blamed him for the accident, he had gone through a long bout with depression. Barbara tried to get out of that date but could not reach him to cancel. There he was at the door, and off they went to dinner and a movie. She got home as soon as she could and vowed not to do that again. Will did not give up. The thing that began to appeal to Barbara was that he was so good with her children. Will had a little girl who was being cared for by her maternal grandparents. Will and Barbara eventually decided to marry. They adopted each other's children. Jody and Shane were Barbara's. Amy was Will's daughter. Some years later, they had a son, Scott.

There were the normal trials that come with raising children, adjusting to new authority figures and all that goes with this part of life, but they managed to survive.

Will was a big man who had a gentle spirit. He was a born clown and kept us all entertained when we visited together. You never knew what he was going to say or do. We all loved him very much. When he was about forty-seven, he began to feel like he was not up to par. After tests were run, the diagnosis was melanoma cancer. It was internal and spreading with a vengeance.

A call came from Jody asking me if I could come to Jackson and see if I could get through to him. He was so depressed, and there was no light at the end of the tunnel. I made the trip and was so glad to hear him say that he was hoping that I would come. I don't know what it was except that he felt free to talk to me about his fears. I think he was still trying to protect Barbara and the children. It was like watching someone die daily. Life was leaving his body so fast. This was much different from Sonny's lingering cancer.

Will was dead in three weeks. He was in intensive care the

last few days. When nothing else could be done, they moved him to a private room so that his family could be with him. Barbara was there the last night. There was an awful storm raging outside. But there was peace in that room. In a period of communion with God, Barbara knew it was time for Will to go on to be with the Lord. A loud clap of thunder sounded, and he was absent from the body and present with Jesus.

The difference in the experience of her first husband's death and that of her second husband's death had everything to do with Barbara's personal walk with Jesus Christ. She knew this time that she would be able to walk through this trial in victory. Were circumstances any different? *No!* She was different. This time she had three children to take care of, even though they were older. There was very little insurance money because they had not thought much about Will dying so young.

Barbara had left her job in the law firm a good many years earlier. She started keeping children in her home. She was so gifted in this area; it was not long before many parents were trying everything to get their children under her care. She has a wonderful ability to organize, discipline, entertain, teach, and most of all, to love these little ones. It is no wonder that they all love her so deeply.

Through the years, she has come to realize that this was her God-ordained ministry. She has had many Jewish, Buddhist, Muslim, and Christian children, and some who profess no faith in any religion. When the parents come to Barbara for the initial interview, she tells them that they can look at her home and tell that she is a Christian. She makes it clear that she will talk about Jesus; they will ask the blessing before they eat; and that she will read them a Bible story before their naptime. They all still want Miss Barbara to care for their children. At Christmas time, I am always impressed with the party she gives for the children and their parents and grandparents. Her breakfast room is turned into Bethlehem. The children act out the true Christmas story. Along with this, they also act out Hanukkah. They sing Christmas carols and they sing Hebrew songs. This has been a wonderful way to teach little children how to understand each other and the differences in how we are all raised. There have been children who have reached a place where they expressed their desire for Jesus to come into their lives. Barbara has been faithful to lead these little ones to Jesus. At the same time, she has taught them not to use this as an excuse to be disobedient or disrespectful of their parents or grandparents.

Before dawn one Saturday morning, Barbara was awakened with some frightening symptoms. She had chest pains, nausea, and cold sweats. Without going into all the things that followed, let me just say that Scott took her to an emergency room. After tests were run, she was released. One week later, she woke up again on a Saturday morning with the same symptoms. This time she was taken to another hospital. A catherization was done, followed by angioplasty. On the way back to her room, the balloon went out. They turned her around and went back and did the angioplasty the second time. She was released from the hospital soon after. One week later, again on a Saturday morning, she felt a sensation like a balloon having all the air let out of it. She was rushed back to the hospital where they did angioplasty once more. This time they left the shunt in the leg, thinking that they may have to go back in. Leaving the shunt in for the extended period of time caused a blood clot to form. Barbara felt the toe, then the toes, and then the foot and then the leg grow numb. She insisted that the doctor stop working with the heart and focus on the leg. She asked if this was the kind of thing that ended up with a gray tag on your toe. They saw the emergency, and went to work on the leg after telling Barbara to quit saying things like that last comment. So she decided if she was going to die, she might as well start singing to Jesus. She began singing "What a friend we have in Jesus."

Several days later, they proceeded with the bypass surgery to take care of the blood clot they found in the numb leg. They had given her heparin, and she was allergic to it. She was bleeding in her mouth and everywhere you can think of. They had stopped this medicine in order to get her to the place where she could undergo the surgical procedure. A nurse had come in to change the drip to the opposite arm. A staff member from her church had come to visit her. Realizing how nervous she was and how gray she looked, and how she had cotton patches all over her to stop the blood that kept shooting out like fountains, he stopped the nurse from sticking the next needle into her arm. He told the nurse not to touch her again until he prayed and read to her Psalm 91 (NAS).

> *He who dwells in the shelter of the Most High*
> *Will abide in the shadow of the Almighty.*
> *I will say to the Lord, "My*
> *refuge and my fortress,*
> *My God, in whom I trust!"*
> *For it is He who delivers you*
> *from the snare of the trapper,*
> *And from the deadly pestilence.*
> *He will cover you with His pinions.*
> *And under His wings you*
> *may seek refuge.*

His faithfulness is a shield and bulwark.
You will not be afraid of the
terror by night,
Or of the arrow that flies by day,
Of the pestilence that stalks
in darkness,
Or of the destruction that
lays waste at noon.
A thousand may fall at your side,
And ten thousand at your right hand;
But it shall not approach you.
You will only look on with your eyes.
And see the recompense of the wicked.
For you have made the Lord my refuge,
Even the Most High, your dwelling place.
No evil will befall you,
Nor will any plague come near your tent.
For He will give his angels
charge concerning you,
to guard you in all your ways,
they will bear you up in their hands,
lest you strike your foot
against a stone.
You will tread upon the lion and cobra,
the young lion and the serpent you will
trample down.
"Because he has loved me
therefore I will deliver him;
I will set him securely on
high, because he has

known My name.
"He will call upon me, and I
will answer him;
I will be with him in trouble;
I will rescue him, and honor him.
"With a long life Ii will satisfy him,
and let him behold my salvation."

Bro. Bill prayed and asked that God not permit any more blood to come out of Barbara's body than was absolutely needed. The nurse stuck the needle in her arm to start the drip, and not one bit of blood came out even onto the gauze pad. That same day, Barbara got two cards, each one with Psalm 91:11–12 inside.

After the surgery was performed, Barbara was kept for a while in recovery. She woke up and realized that she could not breathe. There were three people on one side of her bed and one on the other side, all of them working frantically on her. When Barbara told them that she felt like she was dying, they told her to stay calm, that they were working to fix the problem.

At the end of her bed, she noticed a black lady with a page boy hairstyle, dressed in green hospital attire. No one seemed to notice her presence. She was doing absolutely nothing to help them. When all the medical team moved to one side, this lady walked over to the opposite side. She smiled at Barbara and touched her hand. Barbara's breathing returned to normal. She heard them say that she had come around. This lady walked out of the room. Barbara had noticed one unusual thing about her. She had a pin on her uniform that said *Our God is an awesome God.* As this lady left, she passed Barbara's children, Jody and Scott, and a friend, Anita. Anita asked her about the beautiful pin and asked her where she had gotten it. She simply answered, "*Our God is an awesome God.*"

They took Barbara back to her private room. This lady was walking behind them and even came into her room. She stood by the window while the nurses were getting Barbara onto the bed. After they left, the lady walked over to the bed, leaned down close to Barbara, and said, "I am your Angel. God sent me to lift you up back there." This was the last time anyone saw this precious gift from God.

During all of these hospitalizations and recuperations, Barbara had no income. She had learned a long time before that God had promised to provide for all of her needs according to His riches in Glory by Christ Jesus. She was right. In so many different wondrous ways, He poured out his blessings and provisions, and all of God's people rejoiced as they saw the magnificent manifestation of His presence through the months that followed. Barbara's spirit was indeed able to sing in the midst of all of these fiery trials. The gold was tested. Her faith was proven. The stretched and hammered gold resulted in a ministry and a testimony that has touched hundreds of people's lives.

She is probably in better health today than she has ever been. She is a part of a Cardiac Exercise Program. She still has her childcare business. She teaches a Sunday school class.

She is an avid Bible student. She is a prayer warrior. She is a dynamic witness for Jesus. She loves keeping up with happenings in the Middle East. She looks forward to the return of Jesus Christ for His children. And I am sure Heaven will have many from various religious backgrounds who have seen Jesus clearly manifested in Miss Barbara's life and have chosen to give their lives to Him like she did.

I am so proud that she is my little sister biologically, and that she is my spiritual sister as well.

8. *Heroine of Faith*

Ernestine Wolfe

What joy it is to share with you one of the most amazing testimonies of faith that I have ever heard. Expecting a blessing but not knowing *what a blessing* it would be, I went to Ernestine's home. The soft blue and cream exterior of her condo was a perfect compliment to her gentle and quiet personality. Entering the living room, I continued to be impressed with her special touches everywhere.

After our hug, we sat down to talk about the book in which she would be a unique blessing to many. She handed me a notebook with the word *Praise* on the front of it. "This may help you with some details," she said.

As I read the pages tucked inside, I realized this chapter would be one of the most precious in this book. It was her story in her own words. There was not much I needed to add to it. And so I will let my ninety-five-year-old friend share personally with each one of you who reads her story. So now let's read her words.

I was born in Cheyenne, Wyoming in 1903, the fifth child in a family of six, three boys and three girls. At the age of four, my family moved to Lincoln, Nebraska, because of its fine school system and the University of Nebraska was located there.

I grew up in a Christian home and attended Westminster Presbyterian Church. Mother diligently read the Bible to her children each evening by the light of a gas lamp. When I was ten years old, Mother led me to the Lord, and I joined the church. I remember how happy I was! I had been baptized (sprinkled) when I was a baby.

Many years ago I was back in Lincoln and went to that church to see the exact date that I joined. It was a real coincidence that the date was April sixth which was the date my daughter, Joann, was born. In the record it said that Ernestine Black accepted the Lord Jesus Christ as her personal Savior on April 6, 1913.

I grew up in Lincoln and was active in the church until I was married and moved away. I met my husband, Ray Wolfe, at the University where he was in Law School and I was in Teacher's College preparing to be a teacher. After he was graduated, we went to Alaska in 1927 in the Indian Service where he was principal and I was a teacher in the Indian schools.

We were in the Indian village of Klawock when Joann was a baby. Ray had to take a business trip to Ketchikan and just after he left a terrible storm came up. He was on an Indian fishing boat. Those storms in Alaska last for many days. I had no word from him. We kept getting reports of boats that had gone on the rocks and were lost. By that time I was frantic and turned to the Lord. I said, "Dear Lord, if you will bring him home, I'll do anything you ask." A couple of days after that an Indian boy came running to my house and said, "Mr. Wolfe is back! I told him to stay with the baby and I went down to the dock to meet him. He had been gone about ten days. The Indians on the boat knew of a place called Hole in the Wall where they had gone to wait out the storm. I couldn't praise and thank the Lord enough!

Those Indian fishing boats had no radios, were not very big, but were seaworthy. They always smelled of gasoline, coffee and sweet rolls, which always made me seasick. I would rather have an Indian for a pilot than anyone else because they really know the weather and the sea. Ray slept on a bench with his overcoat on.

We lived in Alaska for almost twenty years – six years in three different Indian villages, seven years in Sitka, and the rest of the time in Juneau. The next move was to Long Beach, California. We joined the Grace Brethren Church and that is where Ray and I were baptized by immersion. They dip three times –one each for the Father, the Son, and the Holy Ghost.

About twelve years ago, (1982), my husband became ill with severe dementia, which was very much like Alzheimer's disease. It was a gradual beginning but got worse as time went on. It came to the place where I couldn't take him any place and couldn't leave him alone even to go to the market. At a time like that your friends desert you and even California relatives never came to help me. They prayed for me but never came to help. I was like a prisoner in my own home. Through all this, I was closer to the Lord than I had ever been. I was reading my Bible all of the time looking for verses to comfort me. The Psalms are full of them. The saturation of my mind with God's Word has kept me from depression no matter what the circumstances were.

Seven years ago I came to the place where I could not take care of Ray alone any longer, so I called Joann. She and her family lived in

Huntsville, Alabama. She flew out to California and said, "Now is the time to move," and I agreed with her. We put my house up for sale. It sold in four days. I got the listing price and I got cash. That was a miracle - only the Lord's doing. I gave Him all the praise!

We couldn't take Ray to Huntsville by plane because the last time we were on a plane; he would not fasten his seat belt and caused a scene. My son-in-law, Dr. Tom Long, said he would come out and get us. This was Saturday and we were leaving on Tuesday.

I said, "What am I going to do with my car?" It's too late to advertise." So I drove over to a filling station nearby and asked if they knew anyone who wanted to buy my car.

He said, "I think I do. I'll call him right now and make an appointment."

He came the next day and said that was just the kind of a car he was looking for.

I said, "Do you want to drive it?" He said, "No, I'll take it," and he paid me cash. There again was a miracle. It was the Lord's doing and I couldn't praise Him enough!

We had stayed in a motel after the movers left. As we were leaving town we drove past out dear home where we had lived for forty years. I had no regrets in leaving there. See how the Lord prepares you for a time like that? There again I couldn't praise Him and thank Him enough. I haven't missed California at all. I had dear friends there that I hear from but I've made so many new friends here that I love so much.

A year after moving to Huntsville, I went to the doctor for a checkup and he told me I had a lump in my breast. I was alone and I was shocked. When I got in my car, I began to cry. Then I thought this won't help so I just looked up and said, "Lord, I'm in your hands - whatever happens is Your Will and that is what I want." He took all the fear away. I had no fear! I had a mastectomy and no pain. The lymph nodes were all negative. The doctor said, "No treatment is necessary. Just enjoy life." The next year I had surgery for a stoppage due to adhesions years ago after surgery. Still no fear!

The next year I had colon cancer. I still had no fear at all and came through surgery without any pain. They asked if I wanted pain pills, and I told them I had no pain. Again the lymph nodes were all negative and the doctors said, "No treatment. Just enjoy life."

That is just what I am doing. I am happier than I have ever been and life seems to be better all the time. I love my family, my church (Whitesburg Baptist Church), which by the way is where my daughter, Joann, was the pianist for many years, my friends and most of all serving the Lord where I can. I had never lived in the South before and I love it. People are so friendly and courteous.

My husband was in Big Spring Manor nursing home here in Huntsville for three and a half years where he had good care; I went to see him every day until he passed away four years ago, 1990, at the age of ninety-four. When we were married he said to me, "My job is to keep you smiling," and that is just what he did. Our marriage lasted sixty-seven years.

That ended what Ernestine had written. I need to add a postscript bringing you up to date. In December of 1996, Ernestine discovered a lump in her other breast. One thing may be of particular interest. Before each mastectomy, she called her pastor, Jimmy Jackson, and asked to be anointed with oil before the surgeries. Claiming James 5:14, Dr. Jackson gathered Bro. Dick Thomassian, Bro. Emerson Lyle, Perry Calvert and Jerry Fenimore to pray for her. Dr. Jackson anointed her with oil, and God gave her *His peace and delivered her from pain.* The Christian surgeon,

Dr. Lancaster, surgically removed each of the cancers. Because of her commitment to checkups every four months, these cancers were detected early enough to not be pervasive. Ernestine had the second mastectomy. Dr. Lancaster gave her the good report that there were no cancerous cells in the outlying area. He then told her that he was sure she would not die from cancer. He said, "Go and enjoy life."

Ernestine's reply continued to be, "That's what I'm doing!"

The next day after surgery, she got out of bed, dressed herself, and looking radiantly beautiful, she waited for her daughter to pick her up. She chose her surgery date so that it would not interfere with her Church Christmas parties. She never missed a beat and continues to be the busiest woman I know. She is a tiny little fragile looking lady, but don't you let that fool you. She jogged until she was about ninety. Now she walks and has started a limited weight lifting program. Don't forget, she is ninety-five years young. Each day has a full schedule, including things like lunches, dinners, visitation, Senior Adult Choir rehearsals, Tuesday Ladies' Bible Study, Baptist Women's luncheons, Christian Women's Clubs, Alzheimer's support group, cancer support group, church, Sunday school, Wednesday night prayer meeting, not to mention ministering to neighbors and friends. She still drives herself to most of these places. I'm exhausted just telling about how busy she stays. Is that her secret? Perhaps. But the real secret is found in her focused life in Christ. He is her strength! He is her fortress! He is her very being! Don't you see how the hammering of the gold during all these trials resulted in this godly lady's testimony as to the reality of her personal relationship with Jesus Christ, her Lord?

When I grow up, I want to be like Ernestine! She is a real role model! And we all love and value her so very much!

This will be a second post script. Ernestine shared with me another bit of information about her meeting Ray. These are her words.

I met my husband, Ray Wolfe, in November of 1922. He had already served in the U.S. Navy during World War I bringing troops home from France after the war.

We were both attending the University of Nebraska at Lincoln. He was in the Law College and I was in Teacher's College. He was going with another girl at the time and at Christmas he gave her a pen and pencil set and sent me a dozen red roses. I was jealous of her because she could keep the pen and pencil and my roses would soon be gone. I didn't realize that the roses meant, "I love you!"

We started going steady right away and he soon gave me his fraternity pin, which was a sign of engagement. We dated for nine months and often met in the University Museum on campus where we could be alone for a little while. He lived at his fraternity house and I was living at home with my parents and family.

The first time his mother was invited to our home for dinner, it was a rainy night. When they stepped into the front hall he took his handkerchief, stooped down and wiped his mother's shoes. My mother said afterwards, "He will make a good husband."

For dates we usually went to movies or to parties at the University and at church. One outstanding date was when a group of couples went out to the Robber's Cave near Lincoln. It is said that Jesse James hid his horses there at one time. We had a great time roasting wieners and marshmallows and exploring the cave. We left there early and went to the home of one of the girls who lived close to my home. I didn't think to call my folks and tell them where I was. When I got home my mother was out on the porch looking for me and my father was very upset because I hadn't called. Looking back I appreciated having parents who really cared.

We were married in August 1923. I was twenty and he was twenty-seven. He felt through all our marriage that his job was to keep me smiling, and he did just that.

9. *Grace–One Day at a Time*

The Murrays

Few things have given me more pleasure than discovering that one of my high school friends shares the same deep love for the Lord Jesus Christ that I have. Her name is Linda Hedgepath. Just recently I made a trip to Birmingham, Alabama, to visit with her and listen to her share with me her testimony of faith in the midst of the many fiery trials that her family had experienced.

A few of these testings will be how I will start this chapter. Then I will backtrack a bit before I go forward again. In July of 1976, this beautiful, vital lady got very sick with a virus. After a period of time, it was obvious that there was something much more happening in her body than a simple virus. After many tests, eliminating a great number of diseases, a diagnosis was made: *Ankylosing Spondylitis.* Have you ever heard of such a thing? I haven't. This is a crippling disease out of the spine. It affected her arms and shoulders, excruciating pain rendering her almost helpless to do the least thing such as brushing her hair. The next step was to hospitalize her and hopefully find some treatment that would give her some relief.

Always by her side was her devoted husband, Gene Murray. They had met while both were attending Mississippi Southern College, now known as the University of Southern Mississippi in Hattiesburg, Mississippi. They met, fell in love and were married. This was forty-three years ago. You would love to hear Linda talk about Gene. Every word is filled with love, respect and reverence for his walk with Jesus Christ.

After graduating, Gene pursued his career in business management. Linda said that if he had been simply committed to climbing the business ladder, he could easily have been the CEO of one the largest automobile businesses in our country. However, he was always responding to people who found their businesses in danger of going under. Each time he went to their aid, the business came back stronger than ever. One of the places they lived was Meridian, Mississippi. It was there that Gene met a man who was on fire for Jesus. His name is Bill Causey. Bill took Gene under his spiritual wing and shared the word of God with him. Almost from the beginning, Gene found himself hungering for spiritual things. The race toward the finish line started, and Gene was running. Linda wanted to be a part of this exciting experience. Feeling like Gene had a head start, she said to him, "Don't go so fast that you can't reach back and take my hand."

Gene's evangelistic heart found a wonderful outlet in the Gideon's International. He also has the gift of teaching. Linda said that he strives for excellence in his business and his teaching and in all that he does for his Savior. What a strong compliment from a wife about her husband.

As the many years passed, Gene and Linda raised their two children, Rusty and Melissa. Not to mention others they took into their home through the years.

Skipping back to Linda's illness after they had moved to Birmingham, Gene was giving her his undivided attention and care, as were the children. In 1978, Rusty was a senior at Briarwood Christian School. Having been raised in this godly home, he was personally centered on Christ. The mind, body and spirit were balanced. He had the love and respect of his peers. All systems were go for his future. Little did they know that he was about to experience an unexpected blow. Rusty had cancer. It was in his leg.

I would like to share with you something in Linda's own words about this trial. It was written as a thank you to their church family. You will sense the deep faith and confidence that this family has in the faithfulness of our God.

Recently I was struggling to compose a long overdue "thank you" note for the church bulletin. It began something like this . . ."Your faithful prayers during this difficult year for the Murrays have truly been felt and received." In running this by my Abraham-like husband, I never made it past the first sentence. "Stop, you can't say that! You can find a card with firecrackers on it or something commemorating a celebration and say, 'Let me tell you about this fantastic year you have been a part of in asking the Lord to bring us through!'" And, He did! Praise His Holy Name!

And so we begin this saga with the very loving and victorious 116th Psalm for the saving of our son's leg and life. This is from the Living Bible (TLB):

> *I love the Lord because he hears my prayers and*
> *He answers them. Because He bends down and listens,*
> *I will pray as long as I breathe!*
> *Death stared me in the face – I was frightened and sad.*
> *Then I cried, "Lord, save me!" How kind He is; How*
> *Good He is! So merciful this God of ours! The Lord*
> *Protects the simple and the childlike. I was facing*
> *Death and then He saved me. Now I can relax. For the*
> *Lord has done this wonderful miracle for me. He had*
> *Saved me from death, my eyes from tears, my feet from*
> *Stumbling. I shall live! Yes, in His presence– here*
> *On earth!*

Rusty was eighteen then and about to graduate. He had peaked his high school career with many really nice honors and friends and he saw no obstacles in his path toward graduation.

Then in late January those new words bombarded our vocabulary- osteogenic sarcoma! Pretty awesome to hear and receive, and well it should, for it packs a very lethal wallop!

All the experts in Birmingham said it - all the experts at M.D. Anderson Cancer Research in Houston, Texas, said it - amputation inevitable, two years to live! The tumor was just above the knee and being well fed by a main artery. Growing rapidly and having already broken through the bone, massive chemotherapy was out - too dangerous!

Now, two amazing things happened. No. 1 and so humbling to these parents, Rusty accepted all this from the beginning as if he knew he had been chosen for a Godly task. His faith and courage never faltered and he truly became "a great lion of God," shedding tears only as he got word that his testimony had changed a life here and a life there. And as the hundreds of cards and letters poured in, many from classmates, saying things like, "Rusty, isn't this neat. I've never really tried prayer before and look, God answered my prayer. I'm going to try it again." Rusty's constant request was . . ."Stop praying for my leg and start praying for my character. I wouldn't want to let all these super people down for anything!"

Through our intimate friends, word spread to two church bodies we are closely related to; Shades Mountain Baptist Church of which we are members and Briarwood Christian School (Presbyterian), where the children have attended for the past three years we have been in Birmingham. Well, all these special, special people became "their brother's keeper," and with seemingly no apology changed the words of 2 Chronicles 7:14 to read:

> If My people, which are called by My Name, shall
> Humble themselves, and pray, and seek My face; then
> I will hear from heaven, and heal their son.

They believed it; we believed it and He did what he said he would do!

These two churches spread the word with an impact like war news in the headlines; and in just two or three days we began to hear from churches across the United States. Now the interesting thing is, as we all know far worse and graver things have happened to more important people, but God said, "I choose you, Rusty!" because he was rightly related to his Lord and his walk had become so close and sweet.

All these people began to claim James 5:16, Matthew 21:22, 1 Thessalonians 5:17 and 18 and all those greats; and as this vapor of prayer went up, it literally changed God's mind. For on the morning of surgery, the biopsy came back giant cell cancer (instead of sarcoma) which is far less devastating. They were able to remove Rusty's bone and put in the bone of a wreck victim. He gets to keep his leg and keep his life and they believe he will be walking by Christmas! By the way, he became the 64th such operation in the world in the twenty-two years they have been doing this.

Well, the gratitude of the Murrays doesn't end here. I had to get into the act by having surgery three times since Rusty's. More new words and a diagnosis two years in the making - Ankylosing Spondylitis - a fairly debilitating picture we're told. But my story is just beginning and I've known for a long time, as stubborn as I am that God would have to go to some lengths to keep me straight!

I mention myself to bring out two more important facts. No. 1 - God knows my weakness to reach out and tangibly touch comfort and security, and so He gave me the most wonderful, godly husband who has very firmly and tenderly guided me through, never complaining about doctor bills or my complaints and groans. Gene earnestly believes that the fantastic Savior he serves with such an intimate prayer life will, as he puts it so simply, "take care of it all!" I also have the sweetest thirteen-year-old daughter, Missy, who tirelessly "plays nurse" to us all and, the dearest of mothers to stand guard.

And No. 2 - It's the people again. With each hospitalization they have prayed afresh with that caring Christian concern that brings triumph over agony and suffering and pain.

I like to express it this way - it's not until I become completely depleted, can't utter a sound of prayer, can only wrap my arms around the very base of the cross and depend on the prayer nucleus of my steadfast family, my three giant prayer partners, my precious Sunday school girls, our close friends in places we have lived formerly and the people of those two special church bodies, do I feel that unique surge that comes when He reaches down and touches my brow. Oh, Father, thank you for love like this through your Son Jesus!

The intricate part of each of these adversities is that God has allowed us to add shading and texture to our character; and humbly and tenderly to grow in Him literally to heights and plateaus that we never even dreamed of.

To cap our story of '78 off - Rusty is nineteen now, was not only able to make up all his school work, but graduate with his class, enter Samford University here in Birmingham this fall, live on campus, plus was elected president of the freshman class! You see, as Rogers and Hammerstein put it, we have been privileged to hold several moonbeams in our hand - Wow!

> *To God be the glory ...Amen.*
> *With devotion to Him and you,*
> *Linda, along with Gene,*
> *Rusty and Missy*

Back to my visit with Linda in August 1997. Nineteen years have gone by. Rusty is doing great. God has blessed him with a lovely wife and a successful career. But most important of all is that his faith in God is still so strong and continues to be a blessing and a witness to all who cross his path.

By 1982, Linda's physical condition was worsening. Prednisone was prescribed for Spondylitis. When she would be taken off the medication, she found that she would choke on her saliva, sometimes at the most inopportune times. One day she was shopping at a cake sale sponsored by the Myasthenia Gravis support group. They were giving out pamphlets listing the symptoms of this disease. When she got home and read them, she recognized them as what she had. Gene called to make arrangements to take her to Johns Hopkins in Baltimore, Maryland, only to find out there would be a long wait for an appointment. Linda got progressively worse. This was meant to be. They were told about Dr. Shin Jo, a neuro-muscular genius known as "Mr. M.G." They were able to get in to see him immediately. Finally, it looked like things were working out.

Then Linda was hit with Iritis, an inflammation of the eyes. She could not stand even a night-light. To make matters worse, she had an injection in her eye that damaged a nerve. Again there was so much pain. Her response continued to be that this was such a privilege. God just kept on growing them through it all.

Linda shared with me something of what it's like to live with Myasthenia Gravis. An easy way to understand the disease is to know that the nerves in her body are healthy and the muscles are healthy. But the receptor between the two is faulty. An example of what might happen is: the brain sends a message to the lungs to breathe. The lungs might just say they don't feel like breathing for her, and so they shut down. In addition, the esophagus works like a boa constrictor sending food down the throat. The throat closes but doesn't get the message to open up again, choking her. This has happened to her in restaurants. The Heimlich will work to open up the windpipe and force air through the closed throat in time to keep her breathing. However, this sounds very scary to me. But Linda said she is not afraid because she has her Savior's hand to hold. She knows she is one breath away from Glory. She lives daily not knowing when the next crisis will occur. A system is set up so that she can push an alarm button. This notifies the ambulance team, the police, the fire department and her close neighbor. They can get to her in four minutes and have permission to break the door down. One day, the battle cry went out and the team arrived. They had twenty minutes to get her to a trauma center. The ambulance wouldn't start, some sort of mechanical problem. They put her into a police car. The police car completely pooped out one block before the hospital. The attendant with Linda was obviously scared to death. Linda assured him that she was all right because she was certain of where she was going if she died.

"Do you know where you're going? If not, call me later."

In spite of all the hindrances, they got her to the hospital in time. Each time she goes to the hospital, she says the first thing she looks for is a Gideon Bible. Of course, it is for the purpose of sharing the love of God with someone she might meet there.

When our daughter, Debbie, was in Caraway Hospital in Birmingham after the wreck, Linda was brought to the trauma center there. When they got her back to a normal place, she and her sweet mother came up to Debbie's room. I'll never forget her beautiful countenance as she took Debbie's hand and said, "Isn't it such a blessed privilege to be permitted to suffer with Jesus?"

Debbie, with an equally beautiful countenance readily agreed with her.

I asked Linda to share with me some of her favorite passages of Scripture. John 14:18 was the first one that came to her mind. Jesus said, "I will not leave you orphans. I will come to you." Three things she said she asks of her Bible classes: Ephesians 6:13–17, clothe yourself daily with the whole armor of God. Read the Sermon on the Mount regularly (Matthew 5–7.) Embrace Ephesians 3:16–19 …If we can get His love understood, we can conquer anything.

Gene said something to me one day on the phone that went like this: "Linda seems to have cornered the market on understanding God's love and how to rest in it." What a lovely tribute from a husband to his wife!

Now we've talked about Gene, Linda and Rusty. But I would like to add Missy's testimony to this chapter. She was raised with all the privileges that come from a godly home and material comfort. She is a strong-willed young woman, and there came a time when she, for whatever reasons, found herself rebelling against all that she had at one time held dear. I will simply say that God, in His infinite wisdom and eternal loving kindness, never let her out of His reach. Circumstances had brought her to a place in her life where she had about hit rock bottom mentally, physically, emotionally and especially spiritually.

Her family prayed for her without ceasing. That was all they could do. It was only God who could deal with her in a way that would ultimately turn her life around. Our telephone rang one morning. It was her husband saying that she was very sick, in a lot of pain, and in the emergency room at the hospital. We were the only names they could think of as they had been in our Sunday school class one Sunday morning. He wanted to know if he could bring her to our house to rest until he got off from work. Laddie said that would be fine.

When I got home from an appointment I had, I found the very thin, sick young woman in our guest room. I realized this was my friend Linda's daughter. I took a quilt that our Sunday school class had cross-stitched for us after Debbie and the children were in the wreck. It was covered with encouraging verses of scripture. I put it over Melissa and told her she was covered with God's word. I fixed her some soup and crackers, which she eagerly ate. Then I told her to sleep. I went downstairs, and shortly after, Melissa came down and said that she needed to talk more than she needed to sleep.

For several hours, she poured out her heart. I trusted God to give me the words to share with her in such a time of need. After much confession, she got on her knees before God and asked him to forgive her and give her a new beginning place. Her new life began that very day.

I am so glad to tell you that God has done an amazing work of grace in her life. Her commitment to Him is so real! She has had two beautiful children who already love Jesus with all their little hearts. Since I wrote this, God has brought Jerry Williams into Melissa's life. They married and joined their families together. Jerry has two teenagers. Life is a bit more hectic but still centered around Jesus Christ. For you see, in Jesus, Melissa lives and moves and has her being.

Well done, good and faithful servants!

10. *From Riches to Ashes to Jesus*

Louise Stratton

When I was a teenager, I had such admiration for aesthetically beautiful people. Shallow is the adjective that described me. I was in awe of the high fashion clothes they always wore. Everything was always perfectly matched with just the right accessories. And their hair never seemed to have a bad day. Their nails were freshly manicured daily. They seemed to walk with a certain grace that set them apart from most of us who never seemed to get coordinated in those pointed toe, really high-heeled shoes.

My cousin, Mary Lee, was on my most admired list. She looked like Carol Lombard, a glamorous movie star in the thirties and forties. When Benoit's, (the premier style-setting ladies ready-to-wear store in our hometown of Brookhaven, Mississippi), had their semi-annual sales, Mary Lee would be first in line. She bought stacks of clothes, dresses, suits, lingerie, sportswear and accessories for everything. Sophisticated satin loungewear would be hanging in her closet for months with the tags still attached. I loved it when she would let me try some of these gorgeous things on. They made me feel like royalty.

Then there was Edna Britt, our beautiful neighbor. She and Mary Lee were both plagued with health problems, but it never seemed to dull their outward beauty. Mrs. Britt had the most jewelry I had ever seen. All of it was rich looking, diamonds, gold, silver, every kind of precious stone, and then there was the outrageous costume jewelry. When I stopped by her house to see her, she would always let me try her jewelry on, and I reveled in seeing how much I could drape on me. She was like perfection in my eyes.

Another one of my favorite beautiful people was Louise Stratton. As a young woman, I didn't know her personally like Mrs. Britt or my cousin Mary Lee. But I just knew by looking at Louise that she was one of these really elegant ladies.

Louise was married to a lawyer and had two little daughters. Of course, I didn't know any of them except as an observer. I remember when they moved into a lovely home on South Church Street. Someone even told me that there was a portrait of Louise that was quite lovely. I didn't know many people who had paintings of themselves. We all had lots of pictures, and some were like 18x20s, (we were blessed to have two gifted photographers in our family), but we surely didn't have someone paint our portraits.

I want to add a note here: I found out from Louise's daughter, Georgia, just a few months ago that the portrait was a heavy oil painting over a photograph done by a wonderful studio in Louise's hometown of Cleveland, Mississippi. The funny thing is that in my early 20s, I went to Cleveland and studied with them to learn to do heavy photographic oils. I now have two portraits hanging in my own home. Isn't it interesting how God gives you so often the desires of your heart many years after the yearning?

As my story continues concerning Louise, I married and moved from Brookhaven and didn't hear much about her for many years. On a visit back home, I heard that the Stratton's had some really rough financial reverses. In fact, they had lost about all their material possessions. I couldn't imagine how something like this could happen. How could you live in such a luxurious lifestyle one minute, and all of a sudden have to learn to adjust to figuring out how to make it from month to month? My mother and sister-in-law had gotten very close to Louise. They told me that Louise had an amazing, transforming change in her life.

I was fascinated because I, too, had come to a place in my own life where I was so depressed and totally helpless to know how to find my way out of the darkness. I had reached the end of the rope when I came across some words Jesus had spoken when He said, "Come unto Me, all ye who labor and are heavy laden, and I will give you rest. Take My yoke upon you and learn of Me, for I am meek and lowly in heart and you shall find rest unto your soul. For My yoke is easy and My burden is light." I exchanged all that I was (and that was a double zero) for all that He was (and that was God Himself) that day, and I've never been the same since. Old things were indeed passed away and behold, all things became new.

Now, I had an opportunity to know Louise, not as a princess

in the local castle, untouchable, but rather as a sister in the Lord Jesus Christ. I had to know more about how she came to Jesus.

Louise's daughter, Georgia, was working at the local hospital. She suggested that her mother apply for a job there. She was hired as a desk clerk. She was very efficient in doing her work. But God had so much more for Louise. She was a special light to everyone whose path she crossed. She wrote notes and made potholders and many other little touches of love. And as she shared a little tangible "happy," she shared a smile, an encouraging word, and a love touch with literally hundreds of people.

Mother was hospitalized several times with heart problems. She was always telling me about Louise being an angel of mercy. I passed Louise in the hospital corridor one day. She noticed that my ring had a fish and cross on it. She was wearing a beautiful cross around her neck. With that radiant countenance, she beamed as she said, "Oh, Rita, isn't it wonderful to know the Lord!"

I agreed with every fiber in my being.

We had a couple of opportunities to talk. She shared her testimony with me. She told me that when it looked like she had everything, she was a most unhappy person. To find some peace inside her own soul, she turned to alcohol. Louise was an alcoholic. I would never have imagined that she could have felt so empty. She seemed to have everything. She loved her family so much, but the addiction was something she could not deliver herself from. Somewhere during the circumstances that crashed in on their family, Louise found herself in that dark corner so many of us have experienced and she had nowhere to turn except to God. Oh, and God was there, just like He always is, waiting for her to look up and say, "I need You to do for me what I cannot do for myself. Please deliver me." Now, I'm not sure that those were the exact words that she spoke, but I am sure that was the intent of her heart. And God made something so beautiful out of her life.

Some time passed, and Mother called and told me that my friend, Louise, had been diagnosed with cancer. The disease was devastating to my beautiful friend. But even though the cancer ate away at her physical body, causing her to live in excruciating pain for such a long time, it could not destroy her spirit. Her spirit, sealed with God's Holy Spirit, could not be touched. The body grew weaker, but the spirit grew stronger.

In October of 1972, Louise penned some of her thoughts to prove this truth. I want to share them with you.

The Poems of
Louise Stratton
2-23-'22 to 12-15-'72

Written: October 1972

"Her children rise up and call her blessed."
Prov. 31: 28

My cup runneth over
  Spills, overflows —
From your heart
  tossed in it,
Your heart Love knows.
Reflected in the
  shining spill,
Your Love,
  My cup,
God's will.

~ Louise Stratton

The cave is dark
   Until a Friend
   Reaches hand to hand
And Lifts me toward
   The brightness
   Of the sky.

Only then the question comes,
   An only Child.
   Why?

~Louise Stratton

The narrow way and straight
Is wet and warm
And Long

From silent tears accompanying
The Halleluiah song.

~ Louise Stratton

My soul has worn away
   it's yoke~
Oak, thick.

Worn it splintered, rough~
   Kicking against
   the prick.
~Louise Stratton

A singing heart
   is no one's captive,
Not bound or held
   with string.
It must away
   in major measure
To teach another heart
   to sing.

~ Louise Stratton

These dwarfed
 infertile seed
I've sown today,
Take, O God,
Make, O God,
A worthy crop,
I pray.
~ Louise Stratton

Nowhere do I find the amazing work of God in His child's life to be more overwhelming than in circumstances like these. The fire in the trials burned out the dross. She experienced the hammering process that caused the gold to be transparent. Her testimony proved to even an unbeliever that God's word is truth. He said that even though the body deteriorates and gets weaker, our spirit gets stronger. Through the study of God's word and by way of our desire for holiness, we are led to have no confidence in the flesh but all confidence in the God who raises men from the dead. Through the experiences of suffering permitted in our lives we are drawn to our Savior. There we find ourselves in a perpetual state of adoration and worship. It is there that we find that our spirit can indeed sing when our hearts are broken and our physical bodies are in great pain.

Louise epitomized the broken and spilled-out vessel that God filled to overflowing in spite of circumstances, people, things or worry. These thoughts, filled with wisdom and praise, are her offerings to God, and God's gift to those of us who continue to be blessed by them.

When I visited with her daughter, Georgia, in Jackson, Mississippi, I learned some more things about her mother. I have been told by several people, including her sister, Stacy, that Georgia is a lot like her. I could immediately see the physical resemblance, and after talking to her, I could sense her commitment to Jesus Christ and her desire to be a witness to all whom God puts in her sphere of influence. She teaches at Milsaps College in Jackson.

Georgia shared her memories of her mother when she and Stacy were younger. Louise loved church and enjoyed opportunities to give devotionals. She would carefully prepare them and then stand in front of a mirror practicing to make sure they were just right. The girls were not aware of anything that resembled an unhappy spirit.

Louise was an only child. She, herself, had been the child of an alcoholic parent. We talked about a book I had read called *The Blessing*. Its authors are Gary Smalley and John Trent. It makes so clear the need we all have for the blessing the Bible speaks so often about. In a nutshell, it says that the blessing is the attaching of high value to someone. Every child needs his or her parents to give to them the gift of knowing how special they are to them. There are so many parents who never received the blessing from their parents. Therefore, they know absolutely nothing about how to reach out with words and touch and encouragement to their own children. This unmet need can manifest itself in different kinds of dysfunctional behavior. Alcoholism can be one of them.

From talking to Georgia, I sensed that she had always felt very loved by her mother. But when Louise experienced new birth in Jesus Christ, and head knowledge became a life changing personal experience with God Himself, old things passed away and behold, all things became new; *now she was indeed blessed and able to give the blessing not only to her family, but to everyone whom God allowed to cross her path.*

> *Her children rise up and call her blessed!*
> *Her friends sound a loud amen in agreement!*
> *Her God and Father and Lord and Friend say,*
> *"Well done, my good and faithful servant . . .*
> *Enter into the joy of the Lord.'*

Louise Stratton's spirit did indeed sing when her heart was

broken in those precious last years of her earthly life. She was more than a conqueror and victorious, not just when she had good health, but also when she was in the midst of the fire. As the Bible promises, her testimony will continue to follow after her and will affect countless more souls looking for help in their troubled circumstances.

Louise would surely say to the one in need, "Look up. Seek after Jesus Christ. In Him you will find the One Who is able to meet all the needs of your hungry, unsatisfied soul. Give your heart and life to Him today. You, too, can know the joy and fulfillment that come from having the chance to start at a new beginning place. Old things are passed away, behold, all things have become new."

Since I wrote this, I had a lovely talk with Stacy. She sent me a picture of her mother for me to include in her chapter. Guess what? It is a small picture of the large portrait that I had admired. Stacy was so thrilled over how this had worked out. Stacy expressed to me how she wished that she had taken more time to sit down with her mother and listen carefully to all the wisdom she had been given from God. I hope that there will be a blessing for her found right here on these pages. Jesus will always shine through the beauty of the transparent gold produced through the hammering process in Louise Stratton's life and testimony!

II. *Faith and Fishing*

Jimmy Foster

I would like you to meet two Jims (Gems). One is Jimmie Woods, my brother. I will liken him to a diamond in the rough. The other is Jimmy Foster. I will liken him to a diamond that has been placed in the hands of a Master diamond cutter. The process of exact cutting has produced a diamond that sparkles from many different angles. Jimmy Foster is my brother's best friend. For the sake of not getting confused over two Jims, I will be talking about my brother when I refer to Jimmie. I will call his friend Foster.

Let me tell you a little about Jimmie first. However, this chapter will be concentrating on Foster. Jimmie is a retired pharmacist, having graduated from the University of Mississippi. He worked in drug stores in Kentwood, Louisiana, and in Brookhaven, Mississippi. In the last years of his career, he worked in the King's Daughter's Hospital Pharmacy. Everyone who knew him and worked with him thought he was a "hoot." That's a good word for him, as he was a funny, off the wall, eccentric and very unique individual.

Joyce, his wife, is a registered nurse in Brookhaven. At this stage of her career, which has almost reached her retirement year, she has been instrumental in planning and implementing a most efficient Health Department in Brookhaven.

For many years, when we would make our annual visits to my parents' home, I could always count on Jimmie calling shortly after I got there. Before long, he would be trying to get me rattled about various controversial subjects. We would always come around to spiritual things. If you were going to use words to describe him, they would not include "deeply spiritual," "faithful church member," "student of the Bible" and so on. But I really think that in these confrontations about the controversial issues, he was searching for truths that would help him.

I remember when we were somewhere in our fifties, (that's been a good number of years ago), I was in Brookhaven. Jimmie was so heavy on my heart. I knew, based on my own experience of having been a church member for so many years and not having a personal relationship with Jesus Christ, that this certainly was probably the case with Jimmie. I expressed this to him and told him that I had been praying for so long that he would see his need to be born again and would accept God's forgiveness and His gift of a new life in Christ. The last day of that trip, I called and told him this was our last opportunity to get together. He told me that I could come over and talk to him. It was a precious time that ended with Jimmie bowing his head, confessing that he was a sinner, asking God to forgive him, and asking Jesus Christ to come into his life. There was a change. The wall came down that had kept him from wanting to go to church for so many years. He was interested especially in a sermon series on Noah. It was a new beginning place.

My prayers for Jimmie changed to, "God, would you please send my brother a godly Christian friend who can show him how to walk closer to you?"

A few years ago, Jimmie began telling me about his friend, Foster. He would tell me that Foster was a lot like me. He knew the Bible. He was very active in church. And he was like Jimmie in that he loved to fish. They spent as much time as they could find sitting in a boat, fishing and sharing thoughts, and as both of them are really reserved, sometimes they just sat and said nothing.

A little over a year ago, Jimmie got very sick. After many trips to Jackson, conferring with many doctors and enduring manifold tests, he was told that he had an aneurysm in his stomach. Added to that, he was told that all the arteries to his heart were severely blocked, which made surgery unthinkable. His blood pressure was inordinately high, and all of the above were taking a toll on the kidneys. Add a few more complications that I can't even remember, and you knew the prognosis was surely terminal.

Now, Foster becomes our focus. I was calling to see about Jimmie almost daily. He was so weak, but somewhere in the conversation, it seemed that he would always tell me about something Foster had said or done and how much it had helped him.

The day that Jimmie and Joyce were at their lowest point was when they knew they had to make the decision as to whether or not they would attempt to remove the aneurysm, knowing that he might not come through the surgery because of the heart. If he did not have the operation, the aneurysm could burst at any minute and he would be dead. Jimmie just decided he was going to go home, with or without the doctor's release.

Foster, who owns an auto parts business, felt very impressed that day to close up his business and go to Jackson to be with Jimmie and Joyce. He found his friends in total emotional chaos. He talked to Jimmie and told him that there was absolutely nothing that he would not do for him. If he insisted on Foster taking him home, Foster would do that. But he asked him to reconsider the possibility that the surgery was his only chance for survival. After some time, Jimmie agreed that he would give them the go ahead.

Jimmie told me about Foster being there for him the day of the surgery. He said that he had prayed the most beautiful prayer he had ever heard. God answered Foster's prayer, accompanied by so many prayers that were lifted up by family and other friends during that entire time. Jimmie came through the surgery and some horrendous days following. Over a year has passed, and he is doing very well now. Oh, he still has health problems, but God certainly did give him some extra years.

After they got home from the hospital in Jackson, Jimmie could do absolutely nothing for a very long time. Each time I talked to him he would tell me about what Foster had done for them. He would work all day, then go to Jimmie's and mow that big yard. He would weed the beds. And he would clean the gutters. But most important, he would sit down and spend time encouraging Jimmie to keep a positive outlook. Things were going to get better.

When I started to write this book about people I've come

across who walk so steadfastly and consistently in the strength of the Lord, I thought that I had to make a trip to Brookhaven and meet this choice servant of God. During the time that Jimmie was so sick, I got him to give me Foster's telephone number. I called him and told him about the prayer that I had prayed for God to send my brother a godly friend who would be a positive role model for him, and I asked him if he knew that he was indeed a gift from God to Jimmie.

Laddie and I made the trip to Brookhaven when Jimmie got strong enough to have some company. Foster and his wife, Peggy, came over and we talked for several hours. I wanted to know him better and to be able to introduce you to this special man.

As I have already stated previously, there are three tools that I have found that God always uses to grow his children. They are prayer, Bible study, and suffering. All three of these were used in producing the servant I'm sharing with you.

Foster was raised in a Christian home with godly parents. He shared a great deal with me about his father. He said that they were father/son but that they also were best friends. When Foster was twelve years old, his parents and a few other couples left First Baptist Church in Brookhaven and started a mission church, Halbert Heights Baptist Church. When he was in high school. no one questioned his spirituality. He had deeply ingrained convictions as to moral values. He had no problem saying no to peer pressure. Saying no to peer pressure is something this current generation does not seem to understand.

Many years passed, he married, had children, still very active in church, (Chairman of the Deacons), and everything was so in order. They were starting a revival on a Sunday, and all night Saturday night was given to a prayer vigil. Foster's hour was midnight. He was stunned to realize that when he started to pray, he had nothing to say to God. In deep conviction, he became aware of the truth that he had been good, he had been active in church, he had been a teacher and a deacon and a witness, he had been a faithful husband and a loving father, but he had never been born again. He prayed that night asking God to forgive him and come into his life. The next morning, when the invitation was given, Foster, Chairman of the Deacons, was the first to go to the altar.

Everyone who knew him knew him to be such an honest man, not given to emotionalism. So no one questioned his sincerity. But his humility caused the pastor and many of the people in their church to go home that night and search their hearts to make sure that they had not depended on something that came short of new birth.

Did this qualify him now for a problem-free life and ministry? Not hardly. I will share just a few of the trials this dear man and his wife have gone through.

They had a daughter and a son who Foster describes as the apples of their eyes. We'll zero in on Cindy. As they described her to me, you could easily sense the love and pride and hopes and expectations they had for her. She was lovely, talented, popular, and excelled academically. They told of how she entered many beauty pageants and won some of them. She was homecoming queen her senior year.

She had been raised with the same moral values and Christian beliefs with which Foster had been raised. But something went terribly wrong. Cindy got into a very rough crowd. She fell in love with a young man who had the power to persuade her to do things she knew to be wrong and harmful. When her parents found out what was happening, it hurt even worse to see that they could not get her to see she had to separate herself from this influence. She just did not seem to care about them or about herself. The things like drinking were bad enough, but the thing that hurt her father the most was to discover that she was sexually active. One night, she came into her parent's bedroom very late. She would not let them turn a light on because she didn't want them to see her face. She told them how sorry she was for hurting them so badly, and she knew they would not be able to forgive her for what she had done. She went on to say that they had always put her on a pedestal and told her she was so special and was better than most. She said she could not live up to their expectations. She just wanted to be who she wanted to be and do what she wanted to do.

As I listened to both Foster and Peggy recalling this, I could see the tears in their eyes and could feel the hurt that has remained in their hearts.

Cindy graduated from high school and went on to Co-Lin Junior College, just ten miles from Brookhaven. She still excelled scholastically. However, she fell in love with another man named Brian who was just as opposite from the Fosters and just as bad for Cindy. This young man was *wild!* But Cindy loved him, and he loved Cindy. And they did get married.

There was a wedding in which Brian was to be a groomsman. For a little bachelor party fun, Brian drove the young men to Louisiana to have a drinking party. On the way home, there was a terrible automobile wreck and one person was killed. Brian was arrested for vehicular homicide.

Cindy called her parents for help. Someone needed to keep her children while she went to be with her husband. Foster was at a Bass Tournament, so Peggy went to stay with the children.

Needless to say, this caused the problem between these two families to get much worse. Brian was in and out of jail, and all the legal problems that followed caused what looked like an untenable breach. Brian would not go to the Foster's home, and the Fosters would not go to Brian and Cindy's home. This stand-off remained for quite a long period of time.

Foster's father, (we'll refer to him as Mr. Foster), was admitted to the Veteran's Hospital in Birmingham, Alabama. He was terminally ill with stomach problems that caused him to have to be fed intravenously. Foster visited him as often as he could. While Mr. Foster was well, he had a good relationship with his grandchildren, and that extended to their spouses. He spent a lot of time with Brian, talking to him about many things. Of course, he discussed his spiritual need for a personal relationship with Jesus Christ. He was able to love this unlovely person and patiently lead him to see his needs. He and Brian would have a great time "mud biking" and hunting. This was the same kind of quality time Mr. Foster spent with his son and his grandson. That meant a lot to someone like Brian.

On one of Foster's hospital visits with his Dad, Mr. Foster asked him to do something for him. Foster assured him that all he had to do was to tell what he wanted. Mr. Foster told him he wanted him to go to Brian and get things worked out between them. That was the last thing Foster wanted to hear, but he would not be disrespectful to his father.

When he got back to Brookhaven, he went immediately to Brian. He told him that both of them had done things that were not right and had caused this rift. They both agreed to put these hurts away and work to build relationships that would bring the two families together.

Mr. Foster died after three months in the hospital. His life had been lived in a way that brought honor to our Father in Heaven's Name. He had served the Lord well. He had ministered through his local church faithfully. He had given of himself and his possessions to anyone in need. He had been a role model for his family. He loved his family, and they dearly loved and respected and honored their father.

In his early forties, Foster received the news that he had cancer. The word itself is terrifying. But to find out that it was testicular cancer was doubly frightening to a young man. All sorts of fears and questions begin to haunt you. Surgery was performed, and radiation treatments were required. It is not unusual for depression to follow. And according to Foster and Peggy, this was the worst part. He just wanted to be by himself, but Peggy would not let him close himself off from her. She got right in his face and declared that they were going to go through this together. And they did.

I asked Foster if he felt that God had forsaken him. Or if he felt so removed from God that he could not pray. Did he get angry with God? The answers to all three were, "No." The cancer treatment was disturbing his mental and emotional balance, but his spirit was still absolutely confident that God did still love him and was going to be close to him through it all. I asked him at one point what his favorite scripture was. He said, *"And we know that all things work together for good to those who love God, to those who are called according to His purpose."* (Romans 8:28) This was his confidence; not in his flesh, but in the God who raises men from the dead.

There have been other bouts with cancer and other crises in their lives, but he just seems to keep on, as his father did, serving and witnessing and helping others who are in need, never seeming to think of himself.

My brother told me that Foster said that God had convicted him of something during this time of ministry and friendship with him. He said that when he closes his shop each day, there are several hours that he needed to use more wisely. There are so many sick people who need someone to come and help them. Some need chores done. Some just need a friend to talk with and share something to encourage them. And that was exactly what he planned to do with the rest of his life.

Foster told me of two different people God had brought into his shop. Each had cancer. He was able to empathize with them. He was also able to tell them some of the things they could expect as a result of cancer treatments. Each one expressed to him that they were less afraid after talking to him. He told me about one man he visited just before he died. The man asked him to pray, and he did. Then the old man whispered, "I love you." What greater reward can a Christian receive except the one that God says to you, "Well done, my good and faithful servant. Enter into the joy of the Lord."

I want to thank God for answering my prayer and sending Foster to be such a beautiful friend to my brother.

I want to thank you, Foster, for being obedient to God, and for loving my brother in such a precious way. You have indeed been a blessing and an encouragement to me as well!

I need to add a postscript to this chapter. In January of 1997, Jimmie died from complications due to his heart problems. Then about three months later, Foster lost his battle to cancer and went on to be with the Lord. It's a comforting thought to know that they are going to spend the rest of eternity worshipping and serving Jesus Christ. My brother knows the full joy of worship now!

12. *Two Truly Became One*

Buddy and Ann Jacobs

For many years I have been impressed by the consistent faithfulness of the Jacobs family. They have served the Lord through Whitesburg Baptist Church in many different ministries. All of us know that when our paths cross the Jacobs, you can expect to see a smile and feel an encouraging touch.

Through the years you may have thought that they had no problems. God had been gracious to give Buddy a productive and prosperous career. He has always been a born leader, and has served in leadership roles in many civic organizations like the Heart Fund, United Way, Huntsville Hospital's Hospitality House Board, and others. His testimony has been observed far beyond the walls of the church.

Buddy and Ann Jacobs were blessed with three children,

Neil, Mark and Marianne. Each child presented them with the most special gifts of grandchildren.

In 1985, I was distressed to learn that Ann had been diagnosed with Chronic Lymphocytic Leukemia. All their friends reached out in their own way to comfort them. That is when I discovered a most amazing faith. This victorious faith was manifested clearly in the midst of the trial. Thinking that they had not had the kind of difficult testings that develop this strength, I became very curious to know more about these unusual Christians. I'll come back to the day that the doctor broke the news about Ann's illness to them.

First, let me share with you some of the conversation I had with them in the summer of 1995. When I asked Buddy if I could interview them for this book, he was so humble, as usual. He quickly said that there were so many other people who deserved to be included in this kind of book, he felt like he was not worthy. I assured him that if God had laid the Jacobs on my heart, I didn't think it was for us to decide to go in a different direction. He got the message and gave me the go ahead.

One of the first things I wanted to know was how they came to Jesus Christ. First things first, I always say. Both told me of being blessed to grow up in Christian homes with godly parents. Buddy made a profession of faith in their church when he was twelve years old. But it was not until he was thirty-five years old that he came to realize he had never totally surrendered himself to the Lordship of Jesus Christ. It was at a Prayer Retreat in North Carolina that he said he had a collision with the Holy Spirit. It was like a five thousand watt bulb lit up the place. He saw Jesus in a way that he had never experienced Him before. Nothing was ever to be the same for him again.

Ann was thirteen when she made her profession of faith. She had lived a morally good life, but had known that something was missing in her life. In October of 1982, in a powerfully moving revival meeting, she was convicted that she should commit herself unreservedly to live her life under the Lordship of Christ. This was that time of drawing a line on the past and walking ahead in complete obedience. This victory three years before her bout with cancer prepared her for the battle that was ahead of her.

Ann discovered some knots in her neck, which led to a biopsy. The surgeon took out a lymph node and now they were confronted with the big *C* ... *cancer*. The doctor called Buddy in to break the news to him. He said there's bad news and good news. "The bad news is that the tests show that it is malignant. The good news is that if you have to have cancer, this is a good kind."

Buddy went home immediately to Ann. After sharing this news openly and honestly, he said, "We can do one of two things; we can live cancer or we can live life." Their son Mark and his wife, Laurie, were living with them at that time. They called them in to be a part of this family time. Ann got over her initial sinking feeling hurriedly, and they all immediately turned their thoughts to their need to take this to Jesus in prayer. They turned all their needs and all their anxieties over to Jesus Christ. Then they got up, prepared for a faith walk through this time of testing.

This all happened on a Wednesday. Ann asked Buddy to get in touch with Brother Jimmy, their pastor, before prayer meeting that night. She said, "Tell him that I believe that I should claim James 5:14; *'Is any sick among you? Let him call for the elders of the church; and let them pray over him, anointing him with oil in the name of the Lord; and the prayer of faith shall save the sick, and the*

Lord shall raise him up; and if he has committed sins, they shall be forgiven him.'"

Ann said to ask if anyone would come and claim this truth with her. Brother Jimmy and three other men did indeed come to their home. In faith and obedience, they trusted God's Word. They laid hands on her and anointed her with oil and prayed for God's Will to be done. Peace and joy filled Ann's soul. From then on, she has not questioned that God was and is in complete control of her life. Philippians 1:21 was clear to her.

"For me to live is Christ and to die is gain."

Whether in life or in death, all the Jacobs were
cradled in love and walking in faith.

Chemotherapy treatments followed for a year. As difficult as that was, she never wavered in her confidence in God. After that year, she was in remission for two years. We all rejoiced over this wonderful news. But in 1988, the leukemia flared up its ugly head again. Her platelets were down to practically nothing, while the white cell count got too high. Chemotherapy treatments were taken for another year. Then she was in remission for about four months.

In February of 1991, Anne was hospitalized in a very serious state. A bone marrow test showed it was full of cancer cells. The bone marrow was not functioning at all. In July of that year, they removed her spleen to try to correct the malfunctioning platelets. The family was called together. Ann had almost hemorrhaged to death. She was told that she might not live through the day. Ann's response was that she was not afraid to die if the Lord is ready for her. But she just didn't believe that she was going to die. *Man may have decided Ann's death was imminent; but God had other plans.*

The doctor assured them that it would have to be up to a Higher Power if something was going to save her. Ann assured him that she believed in the Higher Power and also knew Him personally. She was right on. Before the day was over, there was a change for the better. She was home from the hospital in a week. So many people and so many churches were praying for her. God chose to answer their prayers.

In 1993, Ann was very weak and on chemo again when Buddy began to realize there were some strange things happening in his body. He walked three and a half miles daily normally. Suddenly, it was difficult to make it a mile. His right leg began to suffer pain and weakness to the point of dragging it. He thought it was his knees and hip, so he took some pain pills. This did not help the situation at all. He went to an orthopedic doctor. After tests, he was told that he needed to go to a neurologist. The right arm was tingling more and more. He reached a place where if he was going down a hill, even his driveway, he couldn't put on brakes. His mind was wondering if this could be a brain tumor.

The test's results showed that he needed his brain shunted. Now what in the world is a shunt? You have excess fluid on the brain. Like a baby? Yes, and it's short circuiting some messages on the right side. What causes it? Infections. Buddy has had chronic sinus infections since childhood. This might have been the culprit.

Buddy had been a picture of health. As an adult, he had never been in a hospital. But now, within only two weeks, he was hospitalized. After an MRI and several cat scans, he found himself in surgery to get the shunt put in. I was so concerned about Buddy and Ann both that I went to visit them before the surgery. It was no surprise to find both of them with those glorious smiles and warm greetings waiting for whoever came into that room. When I asked Buddy how he was, he answered with his usual humility, "Much better than I deserve to be."

He came through the surgery with flying colors. This crisis was met with the same faith and confidence in God that they had exhibited during Ann's illness. The bad news you get just sends you into the Throne Room of God where He is waiting to give you that complete Grace package that meets your every need.

Buddy shared two verses of scripture that were particularly meaningful to him.

"But seek ye first the kingdom of God, and His righteousness; and all these things shall be added to you."
Matthew 6:33

The second was:

"And we know that all things work together for good to them that love God, to them who are the called according to His purpose." Romans 8:28

Buddy told me that he had such peace through the whole ordeal. His recuperation took about a year. Then he got back to walking two miles a day. Both Buddy and Ann are going to a fitness center and getting physically stronger all the time.

I sensed nothing in these testimonies that resembled self-pity. They said they had not experienced depression. This is because their spirits were so used to singing on a daily basis in spite of circumstances, people or things. Now they were able to know that their spirits could sing even more loudly no matter what bad news might come or what circumstances cause them to feel their hearts breaking. Each trial had taught them more about how to love and worship and praise their Lord. Buddy said he didn't know how to really trust the Lord until he was pressed in to places where he had no choice except to *let go and let God.*

What would they like to say to you, the reader? Ann wants you to keep your eyes on Jesus. Trust in Him. He will take care of everything. Buddy wants you with your whole heart to trust in the Lord in the midst of your trials. He is absolutely trustworthy. You must practice this daily.

When I went to the Jacob's home to interview them, I went around to the back of the house. The lawn was meticulously groomed. The flowerbeds were full of colorful plants. It was like the most perfect back yard I had ever seen. This is Buddy's artistic work. It is praiseworthy. When I entered the house, it was filled with love and a warm welcome. There I found Ann's artistic talents. She paints the most beautiful birds. As impressed as I was with their talents, they did not compare to the blessing I received from having this precious visit with two godly faithful servants of our Lord. I am richer for having my path cross theirs in such a lovely way.

Sad for us but glorious for Ann, God called her home to be with Him since my visit with them. *Two became one* was my choice for the title of their chapter. It is so hard for the one who is left behind when you have enjoyed God's kind of marriage. They had always taken such good care of each other. It seemed that when one of them had a serious health problem, God gave the other the strength to rise up and care for them. They were a blessed team. Buddy is physically weak, but his spirit is still that of a strong man of God. When I see him, it's harder for him to get up from a chair, but the gentleman that he is, he struggles to rise up to give you his tender hug.

I ask, "How are you, Buddy?"

He answers, "Better than I deserve to be!"

And he will keep on with that same spirit until he joins Ann in Heaven where they will revel in an eternity of praising God together!

13. *A Baby's Witness*

"Children are a gift of the Lord."
Psalms 127:3

John Christian Gray
February 29, 1996
John: "Gift of God"

As you know, I carefully selected the people for this book. The only prerequisite was that they had experienced some severe trial and had trusted God through the testing and had come through it in victory.

Audrey Henley shared such a moving example of this with me. Her dear friend Cathy Gray went through a heartbreaking finish to an otherwise healthy pregnancy. I asked permission of Audrey to let me include this in my book and to put it in their own words. So, what follows is their testimony of God's faithfulness to them.

The witness and ministry of John Christian Gray
The Joyful Witness:

Audrey speaks first.

I didn't know about John's existence for quite a while. For some crazy reason, Cathy decided to keep things a secret. She managed to do a good job of it, too! Most people didn't find out she was pregnant until she was about six months along! I'm glad she told me a little bit earlier than John Q. Public. Actually, I had to discover it on my own, and then I had to drag it out of her!

I asked her point blank if she was pregnant, and sidestepping the issue, she responded, "What is this, do I look like I'm pregnant?"

When I said "yes," she huffed and puffed and accused me of saying that she was fat, and then she pretended to be offended.

Not to be sidetracked so easily, I tried to explain that it was not her waist that I was observing but her radiant face that gave her away. She kept trying to avoid the inevitable, but when I finally said, "So when are you due?" and she said, "Oh, in a few months," I accused her of lying!

I couldn't believe she would keep a secret from me that long! And then, after hearing this wonderful news, she asked me to keep her secret. Of all things! It was kind of fun, though.

I remember Cathy asking me, "When do you think I'll start showing?"

I answered her, "The day after you announce that you're pregnant!"

And it was true! It's amazing how long you can go without telling. It was fun to watch Bob and Cathy give the announcement in our Growing Kids God's Way class (we had to drag Cathy up to the front for the big announcement). Bob absolutely beamed with pride. In fact, one of the couples commented that they were impressed by how happy Bob looked. Even Bob's mother said she'd never seen Bob happier. This was John's first witness. Some people had sort of assumed that Bob and Cathy would not have any more children. I think partly because Cathy had such a difficult time with Holley (Cathy would probably insert here that "difficult" was the understatement of the year, and Bob would say "Amen"). John came to give witness to the fact that "children are a gift from the Lord. Blessed (happy) is the man whose quiver is full."

THE PLEASANT WITNESS:

John didn't give Cathy much grief while he was in the womb. Cathy often commented that she thought she was carrying a bookworm! I know that we had an awful lot of fun while she was pregnant. Friday became our day of play. I'd pick Cathy up in my Dodge van (it got to be a funny sight seeing her try to climb up into that huge van), and off we'd head for the doctor's office, Green Hills Grille and various other stops along the way. Cathy felt so good, we actually met people for lunch (that's because John was gracious and didn't kick her constantly). We became very familiar with the menu at the Green Hills Grille, and thanks to James, a great waiter, we were introduced to the best dessert we had ever eaten! Heath Bar Crunch Pie. My mouth waters just thinking of it! Anyway, this was also part of John's witness. Not the dessert, but the fact that Cathy felt so good and was able to be with people. She literally glowed, and her beautiful face so reflected the love of Jesus that people were just naturally attracted to her. It got to be funny watching Cathy minister to so many people (she's by nature a hermit, and would rather stay in her house better than anything!). But John didn't give her any excuses! He was too good! Cathy wrote to John after his birth that he had never given her a bit of trouble. I would agree.

THE SILENT WITNESS:

Cathy went into labor early on the morning of February 29th. We got tickled thinking that her baby might be born on a leap year. Later on Bob would comment that he was glad it was on February 29 because the date would only come around once every four years. Knowing that the anniversary dates marking a sorrow are so hard to get through, there was comfort in that. Yet when you think about him every day, the date doesn't seem to matter much. The way I look at it - it's a special day for a very special boy.

As I am typing this, my mind is flooded with memories of that day. I'm not even going to try to put them in order. I am, however, going to share several very tender and precious memories, all of which testify to the faithfulness of our God. They are very personal, very private, and they make me cry as I think of them now.

(As I, Audrey, was editing this material for the article I was writing, I noted that I needed a little more "intro" into this next paragraph. Cathy agreed and promptly wrote three pages! Personally, I was thinking about a couple of sentences. I told you she couldn't keep her hands off this edition! Cathy says that if she had the computer keys in her hand, she'd strike those last sentences. Nevertheless, it really is good, so if you'll permit me to insert Cathy's dialogue, I think you'll like it. You just need to remember that for this section, the "I" is Cathy speaking.)

"I woke up about 5:30 a.m. with two very sharp contraction pains, and immediately rolled my sleeping husband over to tell him he could not possibly go to work that day. Excited thoughts filled my head today was the day I would get to see my baby. Best of all, I was three weeks early and was getting out of the three longest and hardest weeks of pregnancy. How wonderful!

The contractions were strong, sharp and regular. I called Audrey and told her I thought I was in labor. I think Audrey found it a little hard to believe. (I know why - she is always two weeks late!) As usual, she was quickly at my side, throwing down everything that she had to do to be with me - false labor or not. Bob and I had wanted to stay at home as much as possible and had arranged for another dear friend, Kim Baker, a nurse, to check on me and tell me when I should go to the hospital. As I progressed in labor, I had secret thoughts and wishes that this labor was going to be different - it was going to go really fast, and I was going to just breeze through it - being brave all the way. I secretly thought God was going to reward me because of the hard times I had previously had.

Audrey got here and offered to call Kim to come check on me. I, however, had become shy at this point and didn't want to impose on anyone. Thank goodness Audrey said, 'Well, I don't mind imposing. She loves you, and I'm gonna call her!'

Oh, how grateful I am that she called. I did need Kim.

Kim, too, had left everything and traveled to my home. When she walked in immediately a sweet comforting peace came over my soul. How tender and confident she was. I'll never forget that. She told me to rest and she would be back in a couple of hours to check on me again. When she returned, she told me to go to the hospital. I cried, mostly because I associate bad things with hospitals and I was scared. We (Bob, myself, Audrey, Mother and Daddy) left in a hurry. When we got there, it was so pleasing to see one of my favorite nurses in the whole world, Donna Webb, the very one who took care of me with Holley, waiting for me with a big, bright, beautiful smile. 'Oh, God,' I thought, 'You are going to make up to me for the last terrible labor - You have Donna here for me, and I am progressing pretty fast.'

I labored in the hospital for a few more hours - got some distressing news that I wasn't as far along as I thought. I cried, then tried to recover as best I could and got up to go for a walk. On the way back to the bed, I felt two very strange feelings of pain that caused me to moan deep inside. Donna said, 'We'd better check you right now.' She was concerned but never let me feel worried. Dr. Pitts came a few minutes later.

Dr. Pitts had just finished doing an ultrasound to confirm that the baby was lying transverse and that a C-Section would be necessary. He was trying to put the belt monitor back in place, and we were all listening to that beautiful strong heartbeat. Mercifully, we thought the baby moved. I remember seeing his hand tremble as he tried to find it again. He called for another ultrasound and a second opinion. The doctor that came in was not gentle in the words spoken. (Audrey is writing now). Cathy was the first to realize what was being said, and asked, 'What are you saying - that my baby has died?' (We would learn later that Cathy's uterus had ruptured and the baby had been thrown out into the abdomen. We also learned that this was an extremely rare occurrence.) Immediately, Betty (Cathy's mother) and I grabbed hands, bowed our heads and asked our Father in heaven for mercy. There was nothing else we could do. It was so hard to believe - we had just heard the heart beat.

Sweet Cathy began to comfort all those that were around her. I'll never forget her words. 'It's okay. It's okay. I gave this baby to God a long time ago.'

When Donna Webb, the gentle nurse that had tended

Cathy during Holley's birth, (and by God's design was tending her again) bent down to hug Cathy, Cathy saw the sorrow in her eyes and said, 'Donna, you don't want what God wants.'

Needless to say, we were stunned. And yet …there was mercy. Cathy and I commented later on how we had at times 'imagined' what it would be like to hear such dreadful news and how when we actually did, it was nothing like we had thought it would be. That's because God provided His mercy. Everything was so quiet, so peaceful, and so calm.

Only God could do that. Betty and I said that while it was quiet on the outside, our minds were screaming. 'Do something. Hurry up and do something. Why are you taking so long?'

While we were waiting, Cathy would every once in awhile say, 'I'm afraid, I'm afraid.'

I asked her to tell me what it was she was afraid of, but she refused. In my head I was thinking, 'She's afraid she's going to die.'

I need to tell her the story about the evangelist (I think it was Billy Graham) who was on an airplane that had trouble and they thought they were going to crash. He was terribly afraid. They landed safely, but he was bothered that he had panicked. He asked God why he was afraid and why he didn't have that peace he had expected to have when death came. His answer was that it wasn't his time to die! I thought if I told her that, it might comfort her. But I couldn't get her to tell me why she was afraid, and I was afraid to tell her the story for fear she wasn't thinking about dying, and then she would. Oh me, sometimes we are too sensitive! She told me later that 'dying' was exactly what she was thinking. I then told her the story, and we both laughed.

Bob went into surgery with Cathy. Even as they were taking

her into surgery, we still held out hope that they were wrong. They moved Kenny and Betty (Cathy's parents) and me to a room that was right across from recovery and that had a little more privacy. Kenny prayed, and his first words were, 'Lord Jesus, I want to thank you …'

My friends, you haven't worshipped until you are able to praise Him in the midst of your sorrow. Later on, Kenny said, 'God has always been good to me, and though I don't understand this, I know it must be for good.'

Betty nodded in agreement and said, 'Remember Rob's prayer? God is good, God is good, God is good. Amen.'

The nurses that helped us move to another room were so compassionate. One of them said, 'I'm so sorry. This is just your worst nightmare realized.'

Betty smiled gently and responded, 'No, it's not the worst.'

Oh how right she was. Bob and I believe that Cathy could have died. Certainly there could have been more complications from the ruptured uterus if John had not moved to a transverse position. I have often wondered if perhaps John laid down his life for his mother. No greater love …no greater witness. And friends, even if Cathy had died, it would not have been the worst. Eternity separated from God would be the worst.

The door opened, and Bob, dressed in surgical clothes, stepped in holding a small bundle wrapped in blankets. As he announced, "We had a boy," he began to weep. Yet, he managed to say almost in the same breath, 'But God gives a peace; God gives a peace.'

Oh, it still hurts to remember this. I was so glad Bob could cry. He was having to be so strong (and would have to be in the days to come as well.) He asked us if we wanted to hold him,

and of course we did. Betty took him first, and we pulled back
the blankets to see how beautiful he was. Our tears ran so freely
that it was hard to see …curly red hair …deep set eyes …furrowed brow …huge hands …precious nose …he looked like he
was asleep and would just wake at any moment. How we longed
to hear him cry.

We held him for hours. Each taking our turn, wanting things
to be different, yet accepting that 'this was the will of God concerning us.'

Having confidence that we knew where he was, Kenny kept
saying, 'We wouldn't want him back. We wouldn't want him back.'

But sometimes I did.

Cathy had asked us not to call people until she and Bob
could tell their children. We spent a long night just to ourselves.
I remember asking God to please burden people to pray for us.
Please ask them to pray. Bob held his son and composed poetry
in his head. He would dictate, and I would write. Those poems
became the most poignant part of John's funeral. I don't think
anyone will ever forget how Bob shared those poems, walked
over and kissed John, and gently laid the poetry beside his precious son.

While Cathy was still in recovery, Bob and I had a discussion
about what his name would be. He was leaving it up to Cathy, but
he just wondered if she wanted to use the names she had picked
out, or if she wanted to save them in case they had another son.
I knew what it would be though. She had always said that she
wanted to name a son John Christian. John, in honor of John
McArthur (an outstanding pastor and author), and Christian in
honor of the main character in *Pilgrim's Progress*. She was pretty
set on this name when Holley was born. In fact, she was just sure

Holley was a boy, and called the baby John the whole time she was pregnant. Surprise!

Toward the end of the pregnancy with John, she started discussing boy names other than John. I remember one time saying, 'I thought you wanted to name him John Christian if he was a boy. Have you changed your mind?'

She just invoked the wonderful excuse of 'I'm pregnant. I don't know.'

I mentioned John Christian to Bob, and he said, 'Well, we'll see when she wakes up.'

Donna Webb came in and said Bob could go be with her, that she was awake. When Bob left, Donna whispered, 'His name is John Christian.'

I just smiled.

Dr. Bailey, the high-risk doctor, came in to see Bob and Cathy. I don't think I've ever heard or seen a more gentle, compassionate man. I remember him placing his big hands on John's little head, almost as if giving him a blessing, and whispering, 'Dear, Jesus, it's so very, very sad.'

I believe he cried with us that night.

One time I was all alone with John Christian. Bob was sitting with Cathy in recovery, and Kenny and Betty had gone to take a walk. It was so quiet, so incredibly quiet. I do not think I could have hurt more if it had been my own son. I still feel that way. I remember trying to pay attention to his features so that I could recall them for Cathy. I remember praying, "Even so, come quickly."

Holding John was strangely comforting to me. By holding him, I was able to say good-bye to a son I never saw or held. Thirteen years of wondering, of sorrow, of 'empty arms syndrome' were laid to rest with John in my arms. Thank you, John, for ministering to me in a way I would have never thought possible.

THE MINISTRY BEGINS

Audrey continues to tell their story. When the phone calls were finally made, it was so touching to see the tender love and care that so many people showed to Bob and Cathy.

One of the most touching memories I have is that of walking into Cathy's hospital room the next morning and finding Bob sitting on the floor with his Bible in his lap. He was reading about Heaven. Suddenly, Heaven was far more precious to him now. It was good to know that he was turning toward Jesus in his grief. So many turn away from the One who can comfort best.

I asked him if he had eaten or if I could get him anything, but he said no. I knew he hadn't eaten for a very long time, but when I pushed him to go get something to eat and he again refused, it dawned on me that he was fasting. When I asked him if that was so, he just nodded his head. Such an appropriate response from one who was mourning. I also knew he was fasting with Cathy. She was on a forced fast, following her C-Section, and he was joining her. Now that's "true love!"

Jenny, Bob and Cathy's oldest daughter, came and held John for a long time. She talked to him and told him all about his family. Her bubbly personality was at its best during that time in the hospital. Even when she had tears running down her cheeks, she was able to smile.

I loved watching her hold John's hand. She made his fingers curl around hers, and she rocked him. When Bob and Cathy's son Rob held him, his Daddy said, "John looks like you, Rob." Rob just beamed.

Over the next couple of days, Bob and Cathy began to see how God had prepared them for this.

They had been studying about fear and worry, and had come to understand what it meant to "quietly trust the Lord."

They had just finished reading about Fanny Crosby, a precious woman tragically blinded as an infant. She wrote many of the hymns we sing today. They read of the loss of her child and how she handled it.

Cathy had finished reading a book entitled *Stepping Heavenward*, with the main character's child dying and how she responded (this is an excellent book for women, by the way!). It was this book that enabled Cathy to say, "I gave this baby to God a long time ago."

Now, I, Rita, would like to add a thought for us. Didn't they dig a deep well as they went through their Valley of Sorrow? God has already blessed hundreds of people with their testimony filled with fresh water from that well. Bob and Cathy were blessed with godly parents and true friends. At every turn, there was someone who reminded them through their actions and attitudes that God was indeed in control of their circumstances. I loved the way that each trial brought forth from their hearts true praise and worship. Thank you, Grays, Henleys and Ivys and all the rest of you faithful servants for challenging us to always keep our focus on Jesus Christ. And to John Christian, we look forward to meeting you one day soon!

I4. *Free To Fly By Faith*

Scarlett and Melissa Chandler

I wonder how many times, in our hurry to fulfill our responsibilities, we pass by so many extra special individuals who God would like to bless our lives with if we would just slow down enough to notice them. I found this to be true in the case of Scarlett and Melissa Chandler. Scarlett is a beautiful twelve-year-old dynamic witness for Jesus Christ from her wheelchair. She was born with Spina Bifada. I had noticed her on several occasions wheeling down the aisles of the church to go and speak to someone she felt needed a special touch. She would take their hand and just pour out loving concern. And you could always see the smile she brought to these faces. One very old lady asked me one day where the little girl in the wheelchair was. She went on to tell me about how she had come to her one Sunday and told her that she just sensed that this lady needed a little encouragement. She went on to tell me how that had touched her so deeply at a time when she needed it desperately. This lady was legally blind.

Melissa, Scarlett's mother, a beautiful Christian inside and out, was always there tending to her daughter. I saw all this from a distance, but I still did not know them personally. It was a joy the day that they started sitting right in front of us in church. That's when we began to see how large their circle of influence was. People of all ages want to stop and speak to Scarlett. She always has a smile and a word of encouragement for each one.

It didn't take long for me to realize that I would love to sit down with them and let them tell me their story for this book. They were eager to do so if it would help someone else. So the appointment was made, and it is my joy to share it with you.

Melissa was born in Kingsport, Tennessee, an only child. Her parents were Christians, but she did not describe her home as a Christ-centered home. Her mother was the dominant personality, and her father chose to take a back seat to keep the peace.

She married Jim Chandler, career military, West Point Grad. Although they were very different in so many ways, she believed that their marriage would indeed last as they had vowed until death parted them. Early in the marriage, she went through her first pregnancy. It went full term, but the baby was stillborn. The chilling report was death due to Spina Bifida.

The second pregnancy delivered a beautiful little pink-skinned girl. November 1, 1985, was the birthday of Scarlett. The good news was that she was alive. The bad news was that she, too, was born with Spina Bifida. This means that the spine did not connect at some point. There was a literal hole in her back where spinal fluid was oozing out. Now Jim was stationed in

Panama at this time. Melissa said very few white babies were born in the hospital there. She went to the nursery. Their little pink baby was surrounded by dark brown skinned Indian babies. What a stark contrast!

Ten days after her birth, Scarlett flew by Medivac to Walter Reed Army Medical Center in Maryland. Many doctors surrounded her bed. The CAT scan showed brain damage. They put a shunt in her head to drain the fluid off her brain. They concluded that the wisest thing Jim and Melissa could do was to institutionalize their baby. It took no time at all for Melissa to answer them. God had given them this baby. They would take her home with them to love and to care for as long as God permitted. And that is exactly what they did. With all due respect to the brilliant minds in the medical community, sometimes they just don't factor into the equation that God is the God of the impossible. His ways are not necessarily our ways. This was certainly born out in Scarlett's life.

Melissa was always the full time caretaker for Scarlett. A workaholic, Type A personality, Jim's time was pretty well consumed. He moved his family to Huntsville, Alabama, because of one job offer that had insurance that covered a pre-existing condition. That's how they happened to end up at Whitesburg Baptist Church, where they all became very active. But the endless demands of each individual's time and strength began to put distance between Jim and Melissa. Jim got his self-aggrandizement from his career and emphasis on keeping his body fit. Melissa found very little praise coming from keeping the house and taking care of Scarlett's need. Although this was totally exhausting, she never lost sight of the fact that God had blessed them with this very special gift, and it was her joy to do everything possible to make Scarlett's life the best it could be. However, at the end of the day, she was wiped out. The truth of the matter is that under these circumstances, it is very easy for each other's basic needs to be neglected.

After fifteen years of marriage, Jim told Melissa that he loved her, but he was no longer in love with her. He wanted a divorce. It is impossible to imagine the hurt and fear that took over her mind and emotions. She was to learn later that he had fallen in love with another woman. He made a choice to break the vow he made that included "For better or for worse" and leave his responsibilities to his wife and child and to go in search of that which would make him happy. Melissa insisted that he should be the one who told Scarlett. She was devastated! How could her father want to leave her? Brokenhearted, through her tears, she looked to God and Melissa for her comfort.

It's been many years since the divorce, and Jim does not spend a great deal of time with Scarlett. She loves him very much and has great difficulty understanding his lack of attention. She wants desperately to see him surrender his life completely to the Lord because she knows that only Jesus Christ can change the desires of his heart.

I asked Scarlett to tell me when she accepted Jesus as her personal Lord and Savior. She explained that when she knew in her heart that she needed to be saved, she went and talked to Bro. Emerson Lyle. Bro. Emerson then went with her to talk to her pastor, Dr. Jimmy Jackson. She told me how Bro. Jimmy had gone through the scriptures with her explaining how to be born again. She knew that she understood, and she prayed and asked Jesus to forgive her sins and come into her heart. They then began to discuss how she could be baptized. She said that was a problem because she had a real thing about water. Bro. Emerson took her to the empty baptismal pool and showed her how he would take her out of her wheelchair and carry her into the water. She felt comfortable with him and went ahead with her baptism. She said when Bro. Emerson held her in the baptismal pool, he asked her, "Scarlett, is Jesus Christ your personal Lord and Savior?"

With my little voice, I said, "Yes, sir."

Scarlett exhibits such deep abiding faith and confidence in God for a child her age. I asked when they first noticed God doing this extraordinary work in her life. Melissa went back to when she was only four years old. It was one of the many times in Scarlett's life that she was having health problems. Sunday rolled around, and Melissa thought it was best that they stay at home. Scarlett insisted that they go to church. She said the people there have been praying for me. We need to go and let them see that their prayers were answered.

This was the foundation on which Scarlett's life was built. This was what kept her going when time after time there would be the news that she needed more surgeries. This was what kept her head high when she had to face the breakup of her family unit when she was just nine years old. The same is true of Melissa. Thirty-five years old, divorced, no education, the mother of a handicapped child, and yet her faith knew that she was still held tightly in God's arms. God would take care of them. Oh, she will be the first to admit that she has had her bad days. There were a couple of months that she even experienced anger toward God. But most of the pain was for a short duration and ultimately gave way to the overwhelming feelings of gratitude to God for trusting her with her precious daughter.

Melissa and Scarlett find prayer to be integrated into just about everything they do. They pray in the morning, in the evening and even as they drive. They spend their quiet time reading God's word and listening for God to speak to them. With their very busy schedules, now that Melissa has gone back to school to get her teacher's certificate and degree in elementary education, she says that time for in-depth Bible study is what is neglected. However, she knows that that is the very thing she must find the time to do.

I asked Melissa about the ministry of the church family to them through the time of the breakup of their marriage. She was overwhelmed by the response of their friends to their needs. Three men went to Jim to try and reason with him. They were not well-received. Different ones came each week through the summer and mowed the yard. Prayer vigils were held. Many various acts of kindness came their way. Bro. Jimmy's counsel was very helpful. God worked through the different gifted people to let them know that His love for them was real and He would never leave them or forsake them.

The last surgery performed on Scarlett was the early part of 1998. A mass of bone had grown on her back, causing her to be unable to lie down on her back. So much pressure had been put on her heart and lungs that it made it difficult for her to breathe properly. This was an enormously tedious surgery and would need to be done in Chattanooga, Tennessee. Without any fear or hesitation, Scarlett was ready to go with it. She told me about a friend of hers who is not a Christian. She said that she thought the friend was going to crack. She was just clinging to Scarlett.

The friend asked Scarlett, "What do you do to be so calm?"

Scarlett's reply was, "It's not what I do, it's Who I know—it's Jesus!"

Need I remind you that this is a twelve-year-old speaking?

This same testimony traveled to Chattanooga and became the strongest witness I bet they had ever had. She was so calm that they didn't even need to give her medication. The surgery was awesomely successful! They had an incredible surgeon who said that he had never seen a worse case than this but had never seen surgery go so perfectly. They removed the bone mass and put in some rods that gave her back an extension of four to five inches, thus relieving the pressure on her lungs and heart. They said that she would be in the hospital for a month. She did so well that they let her come home after ten days. Trips have been made back for follow-up visits. The prognosis is very good. Her quality of life is greatly improved. Once again, Scarlett was anxious to get back to church to let the people know that their prayers were answered. We all rejoiced over having the privilege of joining together to lift Scarlett and Melissa up to our Lord, trusting Him to provide for all their needs pertaining to life and godliness, just like He promised He would!

Well, their ministry is being revealed to them daily. They have touched the hearts of doctors, nurses, technicians, teachers, friends and counselors. And God has just begun to show them all the marvelous things He has planned for them. I asked Scarlett what she would like to do after graduation. She said that she loves little children and would like to be a teacher. Then she hurried on to say that of course that depends on what God has in mind for her. Melissa looks forward to getting her degree soon and having her first paying job teaching in an elementary school. If God chooses, she would not mind if He brought a godly man into her life who would love her and her child like they need to be loved. In the meantime, God's love for them is more than satisfying.

Of course, I asked them to share with me their favorite scripture. Melissa said that she thinks God put the Psalms in the Bible for her. As she reads through them, she finds herself saying, "That's me, that's what I feel, that's where I am!" They are so personal. They make all of us feel the same way, don't they?

Scarlett and Melissa both claim Philippians 4:13 as their all time favorite verse. *"I can do all things through Christ who strengthens me."*

Then Scarlett brought my attention to Revelation 20:15 (NAS): *"And if anyone's name was not found written in the book of life, he was thrown into the lake of fire."* She would hasten to add that John 3:16 (NAS) says, *"For God so loved the world that He gave His only begotten Son, that whoever believes in Him should not perish, but have eternal life."* These are two truths, and they are shared from this twelve-year-old soul winner's heart.

These thoughts were expressed from Scarlett to her mother. "I would like to walk. I know God could heal me if he chose to. I don't always understand."

From Melissa's heart, "I would love for my child to walk, but that has not been God's big plan for our lives."

To Melissa, God's trusting Scarlett to her care is mind boggling. They see God working in so many different ways. The most recent visit back to the surgeon in Chattanooga revealed a special touch from God. During surgery he found a rib that was pushed under Scarlett's pelvic bone. After surgery, according to the scan, all the ribs are in their proper place. God is all over this child who puts most adults to shame when it comes to trusting God!

All my questions were answered. But I had to take the time

to comment on an extraordinary collection of Beanie Babies. Scarlett, lying on her back on her bed (thanks to her successful surgery), told me that she had ninety-one in her collection. She hastened to add that she knew every one of their names. Laddie was waiting for me, so I didn't have time to get to know that many Beanie Babies. Besides, it was late. They needed to eat their dinner and get much needed rest before they started out another day.

15. *Heart to Heart*

Gene and Margaret Kesler

Humility is Gene Kesler's middle name. When he was laid on my heart as one of the testimonies that needed to be included in this book, I thought he would probably leave the country rather than sit down with me and share his experiences. That was not what happened. He was certainly shy about the whole thing, but he put his introverted temperament aside and said that he didn't think he had anything important to share. But if I thought he could help someone, he would be glad to talk to me.

One afternoon after work, he came by my house. He told me to ask questions and he would try to answer them. We began with his parents. Yes, they were both Christians. His mother was Baptist, and his father was Lutheran (when Gene was a child, but he changed to the Baptist faith when Gene was fifteen). However, it was his mother who saw that he and his brother were in Sunday school and church regularly. His mom was very active in their church, even serving as youth director for many years. When he was eight years old, his mother asked him if he would like to accept Jesus as his Savior. Always wanting to please his parents, he said, "Yes." An appointment was made with the pastor of their church. He has no recall of the pastor leading him in prayer asking for forgiveness and asking Jesus to come into his heart. Because he was a basically "good" boy, he remembers no spiritual change in his life.

In August of 1962, Gene took Margaret as his wife. Never did God bring together two more completely opposite people. As a matter of fact, Gene says that the only thing they have in common is that they are both white. Of course they have much more than that in common. Their love for each other and the Lord is very real, and the marriage has lasted thirty-six years at the time of this writing.

In 1971, Gene's job with NASA took them to Titusville, Florida, for almost a year. There they were involved in a wonderful church whose pastor was Peter Lord. Through his ministry, his emphasis on prayer and living the Spirit-filled life, Gene was led to begin each day in a quiet, alone time with God. He grew in his understanding and desire for obedience in his life. He turned over a new leaf, determined to please God in this area.

From Titusville, they moved back to Huntsville, Alabama, and returned to their home church, Whitesburg Baptist, and became very active members again. Gene was a deacon, and Margaret, a gifted soprano soloist, was a blessing to all of us. Both of them taught in the children's division in Sunday school.

In 1985, Whitesburg Baptist Church experienced genuine revival. Led by Bailey Smith, an anointed evangelist, the Holy

Spirit of God turned WBC inside out. Hundreds of faithful members were convicted that they had lived good and active lives in church, but they had never genuinely been born again. It was not emotionalism. It was real and lasting. Gene was one of those who drew a line on the past, not depending anymore on having just had a meeting with a pastor that stopped short of real repentance. He prayed and asked God to forgive him of his sins and to come into his heart and give him a new beginning place. Old things passed away that day, and all things became new. He has not doubted his salvation since then. Gene was forty-two years old.

Let's switch over to Margaret for awhile. In 1976, she began to experience excruciating pain in her neck. Her Christian doctor, knowing her active life, told her that she needed to slow down and get her priorities in order. Her calendar was always full, as it was her nature to try to do "all the right things." However, the schedule left little time for rest. Eventually her neck turned all the way to the right, and she was unable to hold her head straight. The doctor identified the problem, but it was such a rare neurological disorder that he had never treated anyone with this before. He went to work researching every lead he could find. In the meantime, the pain and embarrassment was taking a toll on Margaret. When asked by her Bible study group what they could pray for specifically, she asked that they pray that the vanity aspect of this ordeal would be erased from her mind. Tears came easily during those days of emotional and physical pain. Her desire was to rejoin society, but her will had broken down and left her a virtual recluse. Margaret is such a people person who loved being right in the middle of all that was going on in the church and the community. The isolation was worse than the pain. It hurt all of us to see her suffer. Everyone longed to see her back in the choir singing again.

Margaret went from one specialist to another. One of the medications prescribed sent her into a very deep depression. All she could do was pray and cry out to the Lord, but she felt that her prayers were not getting past the ceiling. She was not sure that God was even listening to her. She suffered with this for almost twelve years before the outward symptoms were corrected.

Three years later in 1979, Margaret felt something strange in her stomach area. They operated and found that the organs removed from her body were malignant and that she had ovarian cancer. She looked at Gene and wondered if they would be able to see all their dreams for their future come to pass. Her heart sank when she thought of their thirteen-year-old daughter, Kristin. Would she be able to see Kristen graduate from high school? Would she be there to help her plan her wedding? Would she get to hold her grandchildren? Fearing doctors and needles, she was told that she would have to go through chemotherapy.

Listen to Margaret's own words. "I had so many people praying for me, and I want to tell you that God gave me a peace that is indescribable even today. I had quoted Philippians 4:7 many times in my Christian life, but now I was experiencing it - the peace of God which passes all understanding. And it was true! For one year through needles and chemotherapy, I had enormous peace, and sixteen months after the diagnosis, I underwent exploratory surgery and was pronounced cancer free."

Six months after Margaret's surgery (1980), Gene came home from work complaining about not feeling well. By the next night, he finally let Margaret call an ambulance. On the hurried trip to the hospital, the paramedic came to where Margaret was riding in the front and told her that her husband was very concerned about her since she was on chemotherapy. Her response was to tell Gene that she was fine and for him to hold on because he was going to be fine, too. Here they were, both in crisis, and each one thinking only of the other one. Upon arrival at the hospital, the doctor, after examining Gene, held little hope that he would make it through the night. He encouraged Margaret to call the family and have them come immediately. She knew her first need was to call on the Lord.

"Here I am again, Lord." She found it so difficult to word the prayer.

Dick Thomassian, their special friend and associate pastor, picked up where she left off and finished her plea before God. So much was going on in Margaret's heart. How could she tell their daughter that she may not see her dad again? They were so close, like two peas in a pod. Kristin was just a teenager and had just experienced the devastating news of her mother's battle with cancer. Now to be hit with this seemed to be more than she should have to deal with.

God taught Margaret a beautiful truth that night. When she was too weak to pray, He had another child there to pray for her. But the most incredible truth is that the Bible tells us that when we are unable to verbalize our prayers, the Holy Spirit intercedes for us before our Father in Heaven. Many more prayer warriors, friends and strangers joined in the prayer vigil. God honored these prayers and permitted Gene an amazing recovery.

Gene's mother came to help out with multiple needs. One of the nights, Margaret felt like she just had a real need to stay with Gene in the hospital and just be there to watch over him. Weak from chemo, she went home the next morning. Gene's mom saw that she looked like warmed over death. She came over to her to comfort her. "Margaret, the Lord has a plan for Gene's life, and He's going to see us through this."

As Margaret went back and forth to the hospital each day, she passed a church that had a sign out front that said, *The Joy of the Lord Is My Strength.* She knew in her heart that He was her strength, but wondered about the joy she was supposed to have.

This was when God taught her another truth. Joy was not dependent on outward circumstances. Joy comes from within. It is released when we surrender totally to Jesus Christ and His will for our lives. Life is not always mountain top experiences, but the joy of trusting in Him can help us through the valleys. She knew He would walk with her through those valleys as well as those mountain tops.

Let me go from Margaret's recollection of this crisis and let you hear from Gene. The first thing he noticed was burning in his chest, especially when he would climb the stairs at work. He went to the doctor and was told that it was too early for allergies (a chronic problem for him), and so it must be acid. On the way home from the doctor, he stopped by the lumber company to get some things he needed for a project he was working on at home. At about six o'clock, there was more pain in his chest, down his arm and radiating up through his neck. This was the time he told Margaret to call the ambulance. Gene, who is a man of a few words, summed this up by saying that there was a lot of damage to his heart. He did share with me that there was a brief period of time when he felt angry and asked, "Why me, Lord?" Other than that, his major concern was for Margaret.

During the six weeks of recovery before he could return to work, the thing that bothered him most was the weakness he felt when he would do no more than walk to the mailbox. Gene's heart problem was particularly puzzling since he didn't fit the profile. He was not overweight, no blood pressure problems, good cholesterol reading, no diabetes. Heredity was his only negative. Both his parents had heart disease.

God did a work in Gene's heart as he continued daily to draw aside in the morning and read the Bible and pray. God created a hunger in his heart to become totally obedient. *Obedience was to become primary in his life!*

Eight years later, Gene suffered another heart attack (1987). This one revealed the extensive damage to his heart from the earlier attack. Three months later, 1988, another angioplasty, and in 1991, during a routine treadmill test at the hospital, they lost Gene, and he was shocked back to life. This time he was taken by ambulance to the University of Alabama in Birmingham where they began Heart Transplant Evaluation. However, the doctors discovered a medication that began to work for him, and he was never placed on the transplant list.

One year later, Gene suffered his fifth attack, and this time, open-heart surgery was performed. Before they operated, the doctor told the family that he would probably not survive the surgery. Margaret had certainly learned by now how to approach God's throne in her time of need to receive the grace package that He had prepared for her. She prayed, "Here I come again, Lord." He was always her source of strength.

Now back to Gene. Undergoing three bypasses seems like it would be too much for anyone to deal with after all he had been through. Not so! He knew beyond a shadow of a doubt that he was in God's hands. If he survived, he would have more time to show his gratitude by continuing to walk in obedience with Him. If this was God's time to take him on to heaven, then that was Glory. How could he lose? He felt closer to God than he had ever felt before. And that peace that passes all understanding settled over him like a warm blanket. During the night, he began to recall scriptures that he had read in his many quiet times with the Lord. Thoughts flooded his soul, like, "God is my Rock and my Fortress. God is all I need!" There was neither fear nor panic, just peace. God has graciously blocked from his memory things like the ventilator misery.

Pain is a daily part of Gene's life. All the surgeries have affected his muscles and skeleton and left him with real discomfort when the weather changes. But he still works just as efficiently at NASA as ever. He is pretty well exhausted when he gets home in the evening. Knowing Gene, I bet he still manages to keep a project or two going at home.

Margaret gets the last word. (Gene would say, "As usual"). When asked how she would sum up how she handled all of these trials, she would say honestly, "Sometimes, not too well." She admits that she asked the, "Why us?" question every now and then. But Gene was always the one who had unconditionally placed his life in the Lord's hands. Gene has been the encourager, never feeling that his trials have been extraordinary. He just lives each day, one day at a time. He is a wonderful example for Margaret and Kristin, and now a son-in-law and two precious grandchildren to follow.

Gene's favorite books in the Bible are Proverbs and Psalms. His favorite biblical character is Joseph. Margaret asked him one day why he picked Joseph, and his answer was simple but pretty characteristic. Whatever happened to Joseph, he remembered Whose he was, and that's how Margaret sums up her husband. He knows he belongs to the Lord, doesn't question or doubt it, just accepts it and lives it! No higher compliment could be paid a man! Gene Kesler is indeed a man of God! And Margaret will always be one of our true treasures! They are so loved!

16. *'Til Death Do Us Part*

Betty Cunningham

Sometimes it seems that we are a culture lacking in teenage innocence. Not so with Betty Cunningham at age fifteen. She fell in love with her childhood friend and married him when she was only eighteen years old. Naively she thought that they would have the same kind of marriage that her parents had enjoyed.

Betty was the youngest of seven children, the baby to them all. There were four brothers and two sisters who joined their parents in protecting her. Theirs was a godly home, filled with love and laughter.

Betty and Jacque married on June 1, 1968. Jacque was the son of a Cumberland Presbyterian minister. He was a football player with those wide shoulders and muscular arms. She fell in love with everything about him from the first time she saw him. His wonderful sense of humor kept her laughing. It was so easy to believe that they had only a special future together. A few years later, they were blessed with two beautiful daughters, Jennifer and Melissa. They grew up and married and gave Betty and Jacque three wonderful grandchildren.

Jacque attended Middle Tennessee State University in Murfreesboro, Tennessee. There he received his nursing degree. At the same time, Betty attained her L.P.N. (Licensed Practical Nurse) license. For a short time, they worked at the same local hospital. Jacque later found employment at the Veteran's Administration Hospital, and Betty went to work at a local physician's office.

Not long after Jacque started working at the V.A. Hospital, Betty noticed a change in his behavior. He was drinking pretty heavily and talking about smoking marijuana with some other employees at the hospital. This was like entering a whole new world. Betty had never even smelled pot or been around people eager to experiment with all these mood-altering drugs. From that point on, it seemed that everything began to speed out of control on a downhill slide. The man she had married was not the man she found herself living with now. Feelings of being loved and protected were things of the past. To make matters worse, she felt that she needed to keep his drinking and drug use from their daughters and the rest of the family. Making excuses for him constantly caused her to become the enabler he needed to live his lie. Betty just wanted everyone to continue to think that they were the perfect family. The burden became heavier and heavier. The time came when Betty realized that she had to fill the deep need she had to be loved and valued by someone other than her husband. Only by the grace of God did she not fall into the trap of turning to alcohol or to another man to meet her needs.

Betty had been faithful in church attendance all of her life. She had never lacked in hearing the Word of God taught and preached. But now there was the awareness that head knowledge was not enough. She knew that if she was going to survive, she had to have experiential knowledge of God. She had to draw near to God and really learn about Him. She had made some new friends at their church, and they were all personally searching for guidance, comfort and wisdom themselves. Their common goal produced such precious fellowship. They began to learn what the Bible teaches about prayer and what a powerful privilege it is for God to allow each believer to come to His throne of grace with every need. For Betty, prayer used to be something the preacher, deacons, her daddy, and Sunday school teachers all did. But not Betty, because she did not know how to pray, especially out loud. After reading the book, *What Happens When Women Pray*, by Evelyn Christianson, Betty's life changed. There was no doubt in her heart that she could always go directly to God with any and all of her needs.

The combination of Bible study and prayer brought Betty to a place of real commitment to intercession on behalf of others. She found herself lifting her husband up to God instead of complaining to God all the time about his faults. She began to discover anew that God loved Jacque just as much as He loved Betty. She was experiencing the amazing truth that God was indeed an awesome, omnipotent God and that He was not only her Father in Heaven, but He was also her friend. She marveled at the scripture that told her about the friendship God had with Moses. Moses talked to God, and God answered him. Exodus 33:11a says, *"The Lord would speak to Moses face to face, as a man speaks with his friend."* In verses 12b and 13, Moses says, *"You have* said, 'I know you by name and you have found favor with me.' If you are pleased with me, teach me your ways so I may know You and continue to find favor with you."

Betty realized that Moses was just a human being. If he could be God's friend, then so could she. This was the beginning of the closest relationship she has ever had with anyone. The Holy God of the Universe was her friend. Exodus 34:5–7 says, *"Then the Lord came down in the cloud and stood there with him and proclaimed His name, the Lord.* And He passed in front of Moses proclaiming, *"The Lord, the Lord, the compassionate and gracious God, slow to anger, abounding in love and faithfulness, maintaining love to thousands, and forgiving wickedness, rebellion and sin."*

Everything in Betty longed to be near to God, for Him to put her in that cleft in the rock and cover her with His hand. There she knew she would find the fullness of joy, peace and love. No matter what her circumstances might be now or in the future, God would be her Protector and Friend and Guide.

This abiding relationship with God was what got her through the next years of her life. No longer could she hide Jacque's drinking problem. Two D.U.I.s were published in the local paper. A public drunkenness charge and two twenty-eight day periods in alcohol and drug treatment programs revealed the big secret. On one occasion, Jacque came into their den at home, obviously drunk and hallucinating on drugs. He pointed a loaded pistol at Betty. Somehow she was able to talk him into giving her the gun, which she unloaded. She felt she had no option but to call the police. He was arrested and held without bond. Betty filed for divorce, and the papers were served to him in jail. Upon leaving jail, he went immediately into alcohol and drug rehab again. The director of the Rehab Center urged

Betty and her daughters to attend a family workshop for patients going through the program.

The Lord did not give her a peace about going through with the divorce. She felt strongly that Jacque needed her, and she couldn't leave him alone. She let him come back home. He tried his hardest for a couple of months, but gradually slipped back into his old habits. They prayed together asking God to help him with his addiction, but obedience to God took a back seat to his craving for drugs.

In November of 1996, Jacque quit his job after he was told that he was under investigation for stealing drugs at work. They were to notify him after the investigation with the results. In the meantime, he turned himself into the impaired nurses program to prevent losing his nursing license. This required an outpatient treatment program and drug screens. If at anytime drugs or alcohol were detected in his urine, he would instantly lose his license. This was very traumatic for him. His nursing license was the last thing for him to hold on to that gave him a future and employment. After taking a few painting jobs with friends, he stayed busy and out of trouble until Monday, April 7, 1997.

This was the first day of Betty's vacation. She was preparing a family dinner. The children and grandchildren were all going to be there. Jacque came home around six o'clock, obviously drunk and on drugs. He immediately got into the bathtub and began crying about what was going to happen to him. He was afraid that Betty was going to leave him. She quietly assured him that she was going to be there for him to help him through this like she always had. Their children all left to go to the store except for their three-year-old granddaughter who was asleep on the sofa. They thought Jacque would go to bed and sleep it off like he had always done. But this day was different. Betty decided she had better take her granddaughter and leave the house. After placing her in the car seat and closing the back door, she turned around and felt Jacque. He grabbed her arm and started pulling her toward the garage. In his other hand she saw a shotgun. Somehow Betty got away from him and started running down the driveway screaming for her neighbor. Jacque shot at her, striking their neighbor's car. She turned and ran in front of their neighbor's house. Jacque's next shot hit Betty in the left thigh. She fell to the ground and saw that her leg was literally blown apart and bleeding profusely. Nurse Betty realized that a major artery was injured and that she would bleed to death before help could arrive. Lying quietly on the grass, with excruciating pain that felt like a fire burning in her leg, she began to pray for Jesus to come and take her home to heaven. It was an experience of total peace and no fear.

As she felt her life ebbing away, she knew what the psalmist David meant when he said, "Though I walk through the valley of the shadow of death, I will fear no evil, for Thou art with me."

Betty said, "I had perfect peace in knowing that God's word was true, and that if I believed in Jesus as the Son of God and had made Him Lord of my life, I would spend eternity with Him."

The ambulance had arrived and taken Betty to the hospital just before her children got home from the store. Police cars and a crowd of people were swarming the place. Betty's nephew, who happened to be one of the ambulance drivers, stayed behind to break the news to the girls. Their mother was in very critical condition, and their father had shot himself in the head and was lying dead in the driveway.

Betty's sister was just a short distance down the street at

their church for a Monday night Bible study. Prayers began to go up to God instantly for her healing. Her sister followed the ambulance to the hospital. She was greeted with the news that Betty had lost a lot of blood, was in critical condition, and was on her way to surgery. Soon all the daughters, brothers, sisters and many friends quickly gathered at the hospital and were on their knees in prayer. One of the doctors came out to report on her condition to find over one hundred people filling the waiting room. He informed them that her leg was the least of their concerns. They were trying to save her life.

After the surgery was finished, the surgeon told her family that he had to amputate her leg above the knee. The next twenty-four to forty-eight hours would tell if she would live. The nurses in critical care told Betty's sister later that after receiving her laboratory reports regarding her blood work, they knew she would never make it to their department, so they did not even prepare for her. One physician told Betty that her blood tests were not compatible with life. They simply had not understood that God had other plans for Betty.

When she awoke the next morning, she was very surprised. She thought she would wake up in heaven! Instead, she was on a respirator, I.V. tubes going everywhere. No one could believe how well she was doing. The anesthesiologist came by several times to see her because he could not believe she survived the loss of that much blood. Nurses and personnel from all over the hospital would stop by to tell her that they had prayed for her. God heard the prayers and answered them affirmatively.

The next few days were very difficult, but the peace of God was still evident. Betty's daughters buried their dad three days later. Betty remained in the hospital for two weeks. She was then transferred to a rehabilitation facility to recuperate and go through physical therapy for two weeks.

Betty is now learning to walk with a new prosthesis. She has had her times when she cried a lot. She has asked God, "Why?" But with God's help, she has forgiven Jacque. She knows that the husband she married loved her and would never hurt her when he had a clear mind. The alcohol and drugs took over his sanity. He made a choice in those early days of looking for something to help him feel good. That choice led him ultimately to a place where he was so addicted that his ability to make a sensible decision for change was beyond his grasp. He could have found the comfort he searched for in Jesus Christ. He chose the drugs instead, and they turned out to be the venomous viper that destroyed him. We become what we love, someone once said. Jacque's love of alcohol could never love him back. It was a false and deceiving love.

One of Betty's favorite poems is *Footprints In The Sand*. It has special meaning to her now because God has carried her through this trial. She has been able to look at her circumstances through spirit eyes and not physical eyes. That's how she sees God at work through it all.

Betty is in the Banner Ministry at their church. This has led her to study the Names of God.

> *Jehovah Rapha* - The God who heals
> *Jehovah Shalom* - God Our Peace
> *El Elyon* - Our Creator
> *Jehovah Sabaoth* - The Lord of hosts
> *El Gabor* - Our Rock
> *El Shaddai* - The All Sufficient One
> *Jehovah Jireh* - The Lord will provide

The Lord, her Peace, provided her healing and led her to the Rock that was higher than she was when she needed someone to cling to. He is *all sufficient* to meet her every need because He is the *Creator, the Lord of Hosts.*

Betty found great strength in the promise in John 14:27.

"Peace I leave with you, My peace I give unto you, not as the world gives do I give to you. Let not your heart be troubled, nor let it be fearful."

Betty's last words in this chapter are for the reader. "Let Jesus be your Peace that passes all understanding. Because in this world we will not always understand why certain things happen to us. But remember God will never leave you comfortless. Only trust Him. Lean on that *Rock!*"

I, Rita, was talking to one of Betty's close friends. Diana James has such admiration for her friend. I asked her to share with us some of her thoughts about Betty. She said that she had known Betty for sixteen years. Through Betty's Bible teaching, Diana grew in her knowledge of God's word. She saw the truths of the scriptures lived out in her godly friend's life in spite of her circumstances. They had learned the value and necessity of intercessory prayer as a small group of Christian friends gathered regularly around the throne of God. Because of her daily walk of faith and obedience, when she woke up in the hospital ICU, she did not find it difficult to keep her focus on Jesus Christ. This enabled her to accept the loss of her leg and her husband, knowing that God does not make any mistakes. He was still in charge of her life. Diana does not question the fact that God will continue to use Betty to bless many lives. Many of Betty's other friends echo the exact same sentiments. Surely the gold that was subjected to the intense fire, then stretched and hammered, covered the altar of Betty's heart. Her countenance glows, showing forth the glory of God!

In my brief encounter with Betty, I can testify to the beauty I observed in her countenance. The gold has been hammered, and it has come forth so transparent that you can easily see Jesus shining through her!

Conclusion

What a joy and what a learning experience it has been for me to spend time with these bonafide victorious saints. I recognize that some are with our Lord in heaven. However, just remembering the impact they made on all who knew them and talking to their family members was such precious time. Those with whom I was privileged to sit down and listen as they shared their love for and commitment to the Lord Jesus Christ were such a blessing and encouragement to me. That is precisely why I wanted to put this book together. My prayer has always been that this would be the encouragement so many Christians are longing for. Can we get through the struggles in our lives? Can we stand and withstand the fiery darts Satan hurls at us daily? When we are in the midst of the fiery trial, can we know that God's grace will be there for us and will be totally sufficient to meet our individual needs? Can our spirits sing when our hearts are broken?

These are our questions. I believe we can see now that the definitive answer is yes indeed! There is nothing too hard for God to handle. He is our omnipotent, omnipowerful, omnipresent, omniscient God of Glory! Praise God from Whom all blessings flow! Now let's just take a little time to recall some of the high points of these testimonies of faith. Since these stories were written in 1999, and it is now 2007, I will try to update you on each story.

The Bridges showed us how to trust God's wisdom when our plans are interrupted by unexpected health crises. Due to declining health, both Floyce and Ellen are in an assisted living home. You will still see them on their favorite pew in church each Sunday. Their faith remains strong and continues to be a blessing to all of us.

Ramsey's family showed us how important it is for us to saturate our minds with God's word when you know you have only a few months with your husband and father who was dying.

Her mother, Hilda, has been an example to her family and friends of one who knows how vitally necessary it is to spend time every day in prayer and Bible study. That's how you can then go out to share with and minister to others in the power of the Holy Spirit. The update on Hilda is that she is limited as to what she can do mentally and physically. However, she is still totally focused on Jesus and His Word. She lives with Ramsey most of the time. She goes to Ramsey's ladies Bible class on Sundays. I see her many Sundays after the class. Someone will be making sure that she gets to the sanctuary. We hug each other. She says the same thing each time, "I just want some of that beautiful to rub off on me."

I tell her, "That's the reason I want to hug you. It's so that your beauty will rub off on me." She smiles and goes right on to the worship service.

And were you as touched as I was at Louise Stratton's changed life? Surely old things passed away and all things became new when she surrendered her life to Jesus. Nothing mattered after that day except that she knew Him in the power of His resurrection and the fellowship of His suffering.

Then there was Linda Murray. She was an example of one who took seriously the legacy of peace, joy and love left to her by her Lord Jesus. These were shining through her countenance even with critical health problems. And didn't you love the way the Lord has just drawn this family into a circle of love.

The morning I spent with Buddy and Ann Jacobs was priceless. Neither of them was very strong physically at that time, but both of them were trying to talk at the same time, each one trying to tell the other one's story. Oh, but they were together when they spoke of Jesus. No matter what happened to them, they knew He would never leave them or forsake them. What sweet faith and confidence! Ann and Buddy have gone on to be with the Lord, together forever.

Nothing was more special to me than to share my sister, Barbara's testimony. She continues to amaze all of us with her solid, unwavering faith in God to provide for all her needs. She just does not waste energy worrying about anything. The update here is that Barbara died suddenly from a heart attack in 2003. So many miss her sweet smile, giving heart, and wise counsel.

The Trent family bowled me over. God is all over this family. Tragedies just turned into triumphs as they stayed focused on Jesus Christ in spite of their circumstances. I marveled at the strength of their commitment to God.

Our visit in Brookhaven, Mississippi, with Jimmy Foster was especially touching because, if you remember, Jimmy was the one "called along side" of my brother to demonstrate the unconditional love God has for all of us. Jimmy Foster died a few months before *Hammered Gold* was in print. I read his story to him from the finished manuscript. He was pleased to think that his Christian testimony would be shared with lost people. That was his heart.

The evening I spent with Perry and Marilyn Calvert was one of the most "enlarging" experiences I have had. I personally felt a surge of personal renewal in the area of faith. I believe with all my heart that this testimony of faithfulness, theirs to God and God's to them, is going to stir every reader to examine his or her daily walk under the strong light the Holy Spirit shines on the Word of God. What joy it is to tell you that God was truly faithful to restore the Calvert's to a place of prosperity. They never doubted His watch care over them. Instead of questioning why God would allow them to lose material security, they stayed focused on how God was going to take their circumstances and use them to glorify Himself in the midst of their trial. They honored Him with their faithfulness to Him.

Little John Christopher Gray spoke loudly to us from Jesus' arms in heaven. Didn't he show us the importance of the testimony we leave, whether it be a few hours or many years? We don't know the time limit of God's plan for us. But we do know that He definitely has a plan for each one of us. So to the parents who read this, make the most of every minute with children God gives to you. They are His gift to you. Speak to them when they are in your womb about Jesus. Then ever so gently lead them through the years you have them in your care to be prepared in their minds to receive Him into their hearts when the Holy Spirit tells them the time is right.

What lessons we learned from Dr. Herman Sollie about building your house on the Solid Rock, Jesus Christ! Steadfastness in that commitment was never dependent upon circumstances being great. He was consumed with a passion to preach. And he was willing to practice what he preached. There is such a need for that kind of spiritual giant to fill our pulpits all across the world today.

What Christians need today is to spend some time with Ernestine Wolfe. She puts most of us to pure shame. Can you even fathom a lady ninety-five years old, a little less than five feet tall, who has never had a depressed day in her life? You might be thinking that she must have lived in a bubble somewhere, totally unaware of all the madness around us. Not so. Remember, she has lived everywhere from Wyoming to Nebraska to Alaska to California to Alabama. Now that's getting close to global. She was the caretaker for her husband with Alzheimer's. She had several bouts with cancer. And through it all, her faith and confidence in God's ability to provide for all her needs pertaining to life and godliness was what gave her the victory in the midst of circumstances much too awesome for her to handle.

We all have choices to make. Let go and let God do what only God has the power to do, or handle all of it in your own strength and out of your own resources. The difference is *peace with God* or therapy.

The update on Ernestine is that she went peacefully into Heaven just days before her 103rd birthday. At her memorial service, Bro. Emerson Lyle read an excerpt from her story in *Hammered Gold*.

What a spiritual legacy she left for all of us!

Blessed is the only appropriate word for what happens to you when you sit down and listen to Melissa and Scarlett Chandler share their love for their Lord. A single mom, getting a college degree while she is caring for her wheelchair-bound daughter, plus all the regular demands of keeping up with the household chores, makes us exhausted just to think about it. But talking to them, you can see the weariness in their bodies, but you also can see the strength in their spirits. They are survivors. Like the eagle, they soar by *faith!*

Friends for years, and I am still amazed at the perseverance and deliverance of the Keslers. God must still have such plans for this family to have brought them through such critical health trials. I understand that Margaret was talking to a doctor recently. When he heard about her ovarian cancer, he inquired as to how long it had been since her surgery. She told him that it had been twenty years. He said that he had never heard of anyone who had survived twenty years. She calmly said, "You have now."

I have very good news to add to Gene's story. His heart had deteriorated over the years. He was put on the heart transplant list, but it seemed that time was running out for him. One day the eagerly awaited call came. They rushed to Birmingham to get the long-awaited heart God had prepared for him. The story goes that a man had specified that upon his death, his heart was to be given to an adult man in north Alabama. After this man died, it was determined that his heart was the match Gene had been waiting for. The transplant took place.

I am glad to report that Gene is looking and feeling great. Sometimes when the wait seems long, we discover that God's time table is always right.

It is difficult to sum up how inspired I have been by the resilience of Betty Cunningham. I'm afraid I would have given up on that kind of abusive marriage. But she is an example of one who was able to see that God loves even the one who is totally lost in his addiction. And God protects his children. No one can take their life if God is not through with what He wants to accomplish through them on this earth. In faith and obedience, she will continue to serve and praise God hopefully for many years to come!

To God be the glory,
Great things he hath done!

Special Thanks

Above everyone, I want to express my deep gratitude to my Heavenly Father. What a privilege it has been to share these testimonies that lift up his Beloved Son, Jesus Christ.

My greatest encourager from the beginning to the end has been my wonderfully supportive husband, Laddie. He has not permitted me to give in to discouragement, no matter how Satan tried to attack me (and believe me, Satan was dead set and determined that this would not be completed. Guess what? He lost the battle!).

Mark and Margaret Tillman deserve my deepest gratitude. Margaret graciously offered her computer skills to put this work into a manuscript form. The times that our new computer just refused to cooperate; Mark came to our rescue at the end of his extremely busy days, and with such a sweet spirit, got things running again. They have a way of making us feel like we aren't even imposing on them. They manifest the special gift of helps and service.

When converting *Hammered Gold* from a printed book form back to an editable document, we ran into a lot of computer problems, mainly with program incompatibility. We thank Stan Sims, Danny Ayers, and Ron Snyder for their expert help.